G000295559

TRADE MY WAY

TRADE MYWAY

ALAN HULL

Wrightbooks

First published in 2011 by Wrightbooks
an imprint of John Wiley & Sons Australia, Ltd
42 McDougall St, Milton Qld 4064

Office also in Melbourne

Typeset in Berkeley LT 11/14

© Alan Hull 2011

The moral rights of the author have been asserted

National Library of Australia Cataloguing-in-Publication data:

Author:	Hull, Alan, 1962-
Title:	Trade my way: share trading tactics that really work, for novices to experts / Alan Hull.
ISBN:	9780730375807 (pbk.)
Notes:	Includes index.
Subjects:	Stocks. Speculation. Stock exchanges. Investments.
Dewey Number:	332.63228

All rights reserved. Except as permitted under the Australian Copyright Act 1968 (for example, a fair dealing for the purposes of study, research, criticism or review), no part of this book may be reproduced, stored in a retrieval system, communicated or transmitted in any form or by any means without prior written permission. All inquiries should be made to the publisher at the address above.

Cover design by Peter Reardon, Pipeline Design <www.pipelinedesign.com.au>

Back cover image: used courtesy of Sky News

Microsoft Excel tables and screenshots used with permission from Microsoft.

Printed in China by Printplus Limited

10 9 8 7 6 5 4 3 2

Disclaimer

The material in this publication is of the nature of general comment only, and neither purports nor intends to be advice. Readers should not act on the basis of any matter in this publication without considering (and if appropriate, taking) professional advice with due regard to their own particular circumstances. The author and publisher expressly disclaim all and any liability to any person, whether a purchaser of this publication or not, in respect of anything and of the consequences of anything done or omitted to be done by any such person in reliance, whether whole or partial, upon the whole or any part of the contents of this publication.

Contents

This book is dedicated to a good friend of mine
A man who works very hard at trying to be successful
A man who works hard to make his own luck
A man who will get lucky and succeed
This book is dedicated to Mark

Successful share trading is about hard work and having the strength of character to persevere. You will encounter hardship and you will suffer losses. At times, you will also get lucky. This book is a road map for those who are prepared to work hard and get lucky ... like Mark.

Acknowledgements

Simon Sherwood

The hardest thing about writing a book is making the command decision at the start to actually do it. This is especially the case when you're an experienced author and you know full well the size of the task that lies ahead of you. Luckily for me, I've always got you to push me over the edge. This book just simply wouldn't have been written without your encouragement and support.

Janice Korevaar

You don't talk much, you just get on with it. What people call a quiet achiever. I also can't quite pinpoint when you first showed up...but I'm glad you did.

Debra (my wife)

Writing a book requires a large commitment, in terms of both time and focus. In order to make that commitment, one's life must be anchored on a very solid foundation. You are my foundation.

Matthew and Kathryn (my children)

Every time I write a book, we lose some of the time we could be spending together. But I hope you can appreciate the commitment both Mum and I put into achieving our goals and I believe this serves as a valuable example to you. So please follow our example, but not our footsteps. Go and make your own...

About the author

A second generation share trader, Alan Hull owned his first share when he was just eight years old. As a result of his early start in the stock market, most of the lessons that the average trader or investor learns during their adult life were second nature to Alan by the time he was 21.

Alan has also had a keen interest in mathematics from a very young age and was an IT expert from the early days of personal computing. Employing this combination of skills and his experience over the past two to three decades as a modern share trader has transformed Alan into one of Australia's leading stock market experts.

Alan is highly respected within the Australian investment industry, regularly writing articles and presenting for the Australian Securities Exchange, the Australian Technical Analysts Association, the Australian Investors Association, and the Traders and Investors Expo. And apart from writing his own best-selling books, he has also contributed to other publications, such as Martin Roth's very successful *Top Stocks* series, Daryl Guppy's international book *Better Stock Trading*, Jim Berg's series *Shares to Buy and When*, and *Wiley Trading Guide*.

But rather than being content as a private trader, author and educator, Alan is also a licenced financial adviser. Over the past few years Alan has successfully managed millions of dollars of other people's money, consistently beating all the major ASX market averages. One of Alan's most notable decisions as a fund manager was to move his entire fund to cash at the start of August 2007, thus preserving his clients' capital throughout one of the worst global financial crises of the past century.

With a focus on the practical, Alan lays it out in black and white in this tell-all book on how he trades the Australian stock market. Like his other books, this one will no doubt become compulsory reading for anyone who hopes to successfully trade the Australian stock market.

Preface

Knowledge is valuable. Either someone else passes on knowledge to us or we acquire it for ourselves, the latter approach usually involving some degree of pain. A typical example is sticking your hand in a fire. I know I was told by my father not to stick my hand in the fire or I'd get burnt, but I was (and still am) the type of person who has to discover these sorts of dangers for myself.

When speaking publicly, I often say that I'm in possession of what I know today because of the money I have lost in the market, not because of the money I've made. I've stuck around because I have a fairly high psychological pain threshold and I'm extremely stubborn (psychology is a major aspect of share trading and we therefore discuss it in chapter 13). I have suffered greatly in my life to work out what does work and what doesn't work, and I've found that sticking my hand in a fire will burn my fingers.

The stock market is very much like life in general, where one learns what works by spending a great deal of time and energy working out what doesn't work. I bought my first share when I was only eight years old, so I've spent a very large proportion of my life testing a very wide range of different trading tactics. I've tried using tips and rumours, expert analysis from different gurus and media sources, piggybacking the likes of Kerry Packer and Warren Buffett, and even cyclical analysis.

Here's what I discovered — all these techniques work and don't work. Their success depends largely on when you use them, so at some point all these different approaches will make you money, but at some point they'll also take it away again. It's like the old saying about a broken watch being right twice a day — unless it works all the time, it's useless. So it is with share trading tactics: either they are universal in their application or they are effectively useless, not to mention costly.

There are a lot of broken watches out there when it comes to share trading, so the first problem any newcomer to the stock market will encounter is the problem of sorting through so many choices when it comes to share trading ideas, philosophies, systems and strategies. To help you deal with all of these distractions and stay focused, I discuss the problem of the noise in the marketplace in chapter 14. Hopefully being aware of the issue will help you to deal with it. To be forewarned is to be forearmed.

Call it a collection of observations, facts and/or truths — the knowledge that I have accumulated in my lifetime has often been obtained at great personal expense. This particularly applies to the knowledge I possess about the stock market. This book is based on my knowledge of the stock market and share trading, namely two key facts that I have come by at great personal expense. I hope that I can pass this knowledge on to you through this book, saving you much of the pain that I have endured at the hands of the stock market.

My two key facts about the stock market are:

- share prices tend to trend
- share prices cannot remain at rest indefinitely.

I know these two observations sound ridiculously simple, and they are, but the reality I've discovered over many years of share trading is that any strategy based on them works and will most likely continue to work in the future. While there may be periods in the market when these observations don't work, they can generally be treated as universal observations, or facts, when it comes to trading shares.

'Share prices tend to trend' is probably the most obvious of these two observations and you don't have to look very far to see this. If you look at a long-term chart of the Australian All Ordinaries (All Ords) index, which is an aggregate of about 300 shares and can, therefore, be considered as representative of the behaviour of the Australian stock market in general, you can clearly see that the market has a strong tendency to trend either up or down for sustained periods of time. Of course, this behaviour is also inherent to the individual shares that make up the All Ords index as well.

Now to my second observation: a share's price cannot remain at rest indefinitely. Price activity consolidates down to what chartists call a point of agreement and then 'breaks out' from this point. Like trending, this is a commonly observed phenomenon when it comes to share price behaviour, and one that traders can easily and reliably profit from by anticipating and then buying into the ensuing rally.

To consistently take profits from the stock market, we need to employ a trading strategy or strategies that exploit these robust behavioural traits. Thus, from these two key observations comes my two trading systems: active trading and breakout trading. This book explains these two strategies in detail. Chapters 6–8 are dedicated to active trading, and chapters 9–12 deal with breakout trading.

Like the observations they're based on, these trading systems are both robust and reliable. I'd also love to say that these systems are as simple as the concepts behind them, but that would be somewhat misleading. A reality of share trading is that some maths is involved and therefore it is an advantage if you are numerically literate.

But before we launch into any detailed technical explanations, we start out at a very sedate pace by simply addressing the basic question of 'What is share trading?' in chapter 1. The story builds from there and while there's plenty of interesting stuff for both the newcomer to the stock market and the more experienced, I certainly don't offer any magic bullet solutions.

In fact, apart from showing you what does work, I'm also going to debunk a few myths, such as the silly notion that currency trading is as easy as share trading, or that successful trading systems have to be complicated and expensive. Most of these spurious notions are put out by product vendors who are the only ones who actually make a profit by them.

This book focuses essentially on observing and analysing price behaviour. Understanding how to read and interpret price charts is critical to both fully appreciating this book and being a successful trader. For this reason I have dedicated chapters 2 and 3 entirely to understanding price charts.

The common attribute of all successful trading systems is quantitative risk management, which we cover in chapter 4. Most books on share trading leave this subject until near the end of the book, but I thought I would break with this convention and include it in one of the early chapters. Hopefully this means that no-one will put this book down before being exposed to this vitally important subject.

While it is not absolutely critical to success, a common feature of successful people in any walk of life is the ability (and discipline) to organise themselves. To be organised, you need to be systematic, and share trading lends itself easily to being broken down into step-by-step, systematic processes. We use a proven share trading system in chapter 5 and break it down into its separate key processes in order to demonstrate this.

The trading system used in chapter 5 is my active investing strategy, which is a medium- to long-term blue chip share trading strategy. This book primarily focuses on short-term trading tactics. However, to provide you with the complete picture of how I trade shares, it is appropriate that I at least cover blue chip share trading in brief. For this reason, the last chapter also addresses the question of how to trade these elephants of the stock market.

It should be clearly understood that the trading systems contained in this book are medium risk and should be combined with a low-risk approach, such as my active investing strategy, to achieve a total share trading solution.

Many books of this kind contain recommendations about what material is compulsory reading and which sections can be skipped. I am not in favour of giving this sort of direction because I rarely include optional material in my books. But that said, a lot of modern charting software includes my indicators and, therefore, it is not entirely necessary that you fully comprehend the details on indicator construction.

This book covers two short-term, medium-risk share trading strategies that have been well proven over years of application to the Australian stock market. While these strategies have a degree of universality, this book does not cover currency trading, index trading, options, warrants, futures or CFDs. Furthermore, the indicators described in this book have been tuned for trading Australian shares and should not be applied to any other type of financial market or product without very careful adjustment.

I would like to acknowledge the contributions to this book by Simon Sherwood and Janice Korevaar. Not only did they both make my life considerably easier, but they also added their voices to the text, which I believe has greatly enriched it.

I hope you find your journey through this book both enlightening and enjoyable, and that you take away from it three pieces of information: markets tend to trend, markets cannot remain at rest indefinitely and risk management is essential for success as a trader. Enjoy the journey...

Alan Hull
June 2011

PART I

A few things you should know

Chapter 1

What is share trading?

To really understand what share trading is, we should look at what the stock market is and how it came about. I am a second generation share trader and before I was even a teenager my father sat me down and explained to me what a stock market is. Here is the story as it was told to me as a child...

A long time ago, before the stock market ever existed, there was a man we will call Mr A. One day Mr A had an idea—a great idea. An idea about how to build a better ship...

But it was an idea about a big ship and Mr A did not have enough money to build his ship. So Mr A got depressed...

In fact there were lots of men and women with lots of great ideas about lots of things, but none of their ideas ever became a reality, until one day Mr A had an idea about money. His money idea was to break up his ship venture and find other people to share in it.

So Mr A formed a company and went to Mr B, who was a good salesman, and got him to sell 'shares' in his new shipbuilding company. Mr A paid Mr B well, so Mr B worked very hard and managed to sell all of the shares. This made Mr A very happy.

In fact, Mr B made so much money selling Mr A's idea that he brokered deals between the other people who had ideas and members of the public who wanted to invest. And when Mr A's company began to make money, he divided the profits among the shareholders. He sent money to the shareholders every year that he made a profit.

One of his investors, Mr C, had an idea and wanted to sell his holdings in Mr A's company to pursue his own clever idea. But it was very hard for Mr C to sell his shares because Mr A did not want to buy them back and there was no marketplace for shares. So Mr C started one and called it a stock market.

And that is the ABC of how the stock market began!

Of course, this is a very simple explanation of how stock markets came into existence and why we have them, but it is conceptually accurate. Stock markets serve the very serious functions of raising venture capital and facilitating the transferring of interests in companies from one investor to another. Here are some additional key points worth noting:

- Mr A and people like him are entrepreneurs.
- Mr B brokers deals between entrepreneurs and investors and is called a stockbroker.
- Furthermore, thanks to Mr C and the creation of the stock market, Mr B also brokers deals between investors, transferring company interests from one party to another.
- When stockbrokers place shares with investors it is called the primary market.
- When shares are bought and sold in the stock market it is called the secondary market.
- Company profits are split and distributed regularly to shareholders as dividends.
- Stock markets also regulate publicly listed companies to protect investors' interests.

That pretty much explains what a stock market is, so now we can move to the really big question: what is share trading?

Share trading—a simple explanation

How to define share trading is a very common point of confusion for many stock market participants, including newcomers and even the more experienced, so I'm going to examine how to define share trading from several directions to provide you with as much clarity as possible. Let's start with a very simple explanation (with pictures, of course).

The fortunes of a company inevitably change over time, so the price of the shares that represent a company's value increase and decrease in sympathy with these changes (see figure 1.1).

Figure 1.1: share prices rise and fall over time

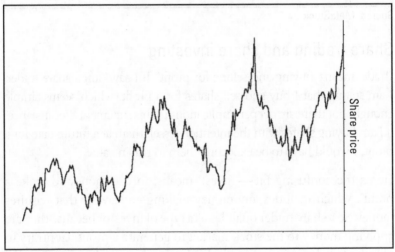

Source: MetaStock

It's therefore possible to make money from buying and selling shares, providing you sell the share for a higher price than you paid for it. So while you own the share, the share's price must increase (see figure 1.2, overleaf).

In investment circles this is given the fancy name of 'capital growth'. It all sounds simple enough, but so often people confuse 'trading' with 'investing', so now I'll clarify the difference between these two distinctly different ways of dealing in shares.

Figure 1.2: rising share price

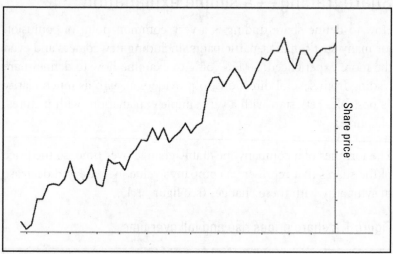

Source: MetaStock

Share trading and share investing

'Trade' means 'buying and selling for profit'. If I say I am a share trader, I am stating that I buy and sell shares for a profit, which seems simple enough, but there are deeper implications to this statement. For instance, if I am buying shares with the intention to sell them at a future date for a profit, I would have to be expecting them to rise in value.

Here's the confusing bit — 'invest' means 'to use money to make a profit', which includes any money-making endeavour that requires money. So a share trader qualifies as a type of investor because they are applying money to the stock market to generate a profit. Contrary to popular belief, a person who deals in shares is not defined as a 'trader' by the number of trades they perform each year. This definition was created by a certain government department and, while it may serve their purposes well, it is very misleading for the rest of us.

If you purchase a share with the intention to sell it at any time in the future for a profit, then you are a share trader. The value of the share must obviously go up while it is in your possession, but you could sell it after one week, one year, 10 years or even longer. An example of a very long-term trade is art that is purchased and owned by several generations in one family before being sold. The same family may own the art for 100 years or even longer, but by definition it is still trading.

Warren Buffett is an investor

World-renowned investor Warren Buffett defines an investor as being an 'asset manager'. Warren Buffett's company, Berkshire Hathaway, is an asset management company that buys interests in companies that are undervalued, improves their operation over time, then derives a return from them via the company's increased profits.

Warren Buffett's favourite holding time is forever because he buys into companies to derive an ongoing interest in their operation, not to sell their stock at some point in the future for capital growth. Thus, Warren definitely is not a share or stock trader (shares are called stocks in the US).

In other words, he is primarily interested in ongoing profits and he views any capital growth largely as a bonus. Warren is therefore focused on a company's profits as a proportion of a company's value, which is a function of its share price. Unlike a share trader who will sell shares that start to fall in value, Warren will buy more shares if a company becomes undervalued (in his opinion) due to a falling share price. So a share trader wants to buy a rising share price and an investor (or asset manager) like Warren wants to buy a high income/profit yield, which occurs when the share price falls—perfectly opposed objectives!

Here is an example to help clarify Warren's perspective.

Let's assume that a company pays an annual dividend of $1.00 and the share price is $10.00. The dividend yield or income yield, therefore, is

$1.00/$10.00 = 10 per cent per annum.

Now let's assume the share price drops to $8.00 but the dividend remains at $1.00 per annum—a not unlikely occurrence given that a company's profitability is not necessarily linked to its share price. The dividend yield would, therefore, increase to

$1.00/$8.00 = 12.5 per cent per annum.

So if you're an investor like Warren Buffett and looking to buy a highly profitable or high yielding stock, the direction of the share price is largely irrelevant because, like Warren, you have no intention of selling the share at a later date. In fact, if the share price was to halve during a stock market crash you would buy more shares because the yield will have doubled.

On the other hand, if you're a share trader, you want the share price to be rising, so you can see why it is so important that you do not confuse trading and investing. While you can be both an investor and a trader, it is imperative that you keep these two different activities completely separate.

Now that we have clarified what share trading is, I want to address the question, 'Why trade shares?'

Why trade shares?

I have a confession to make...I'm lazy. But in my defence, I work very hard at figuring out ways to be lazy (now there's a paradox). I'm always seeking more income for less effort, and share trading facilitates this—providing I do it successfully, of course. Figure 1.3 explains how most of us make money.

Figure 1.3: how most of us make money

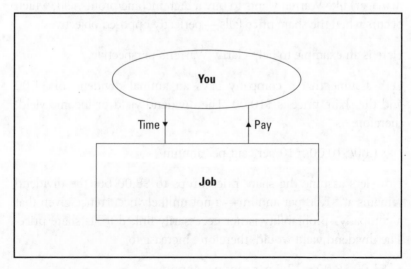

'A fair day's pay for a fair day's work.' This statement was drummed into me as a child and the lesson was, 'work hard and you'll do well'. It is true, but limited to the amount of hours in a day. What we're all actually doing is selling our time, and the more your time is worth, the more you'll get paid. That's why surgeons get paid a lot: their skill set is highly valued and therefore their time is very valuable (see figure 1.4).

Figure 1.4: a surgeon's skill set is highly valued and therefore their time is very valuable

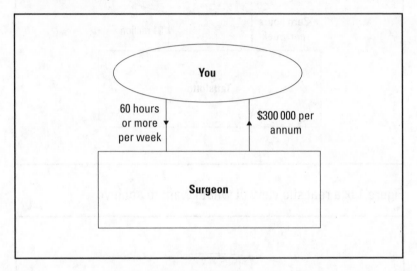

The problem I have with being a surgeon isn't the pay, of course, but the amount of time and effort I have to inject into the process to get the big pay packet. In fact, all I'm after is a comfortable income, but I want to achieve it without having to sacrifice very much of my time. Figure 1.5 (overleaf) portrays an ideal scenario.

OK, it's a little flaky, but as a hypothetical example it expresses an ideal scenario. I want to use my time as efficiently as possible and walk away with enough income to be comfortable, but also have the time to enjoy it. Being a little more realistic, figure 1.6 (overleaf) shows what I want.

And now we get to the crux of the matter... share trading is a great type of business because I can make a comfortable income with very little effort. Of course, this depends on me going about it the right way and not being sucked in by all the hype and spending a fortune on some silly product that promises a lot and delivers little. But more on this later.

Figure 1.5: an ideal scenario for achieving a comfortable income

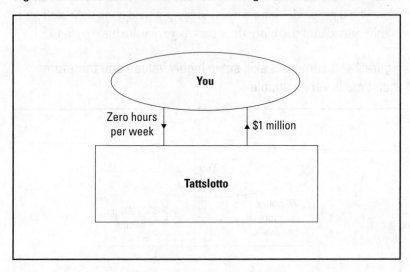

Figure 1.6: a realistic view of what I want to achieve

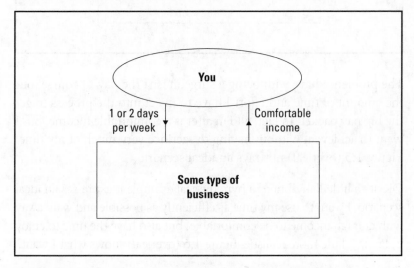

Share trading is a business

I'm often asked, 'is it possible to make a living from share trading?' The answer is, 'yes, it is, and you can anticipate a return over time of about 20 to 30 per cent per annum'. So if you have a capital base of $400 000 and you can live comfortably on $100 000 per annum, you can make a living from share trading. Of course, you won't achieve this type of return next week—yes, it is possible to use borrowed funds, but the risk of ruin becomes proportionally greater.

I don't recommend gearing up if it can possibly be avoided. Let us say you have $50 000 and you're just starting out. I suggest that you keep earning the bulk of your living from another source while you build your capital base, knowledge and market experience. It takes most people somewhere between three and five years to develop the skills and acquire the market experience to trade successfully.

Another important qualification is that income from share trading isn't linear. Like any business that might be earning 20 to 30 per cent return on investment per annum, it does not mean you'll be earning 5 to 7.5 per cent per fiscal quarter. In fact, you may have years where you earn as little as 10 per cent, then years when you make as much as 100 per cent, or even more!

I have on many occasions been approached by novice traders who have lamented the fact that they've followed a supposedly successful trading system to the letter, only to lose money. On quizzing them, I usually discover that the period in question is about three months and they have executed no more than about 10 trades. I tell them to come back and talk to me again in about one year when they have executed at least 50 trades.

This usually solicits a response along the lines of, 'But I need to make money now'. And this is when I tell them to get a job and they decide they do not like me anymore. Here's the bottom line: in nearly 30 years of being a trader I have never come across a trading system that will make money week in, week out. In fact, some of the best systems I know, and have used, can spend up to six months under water (that is, operating at a loss).

The idea that income from share trading is linear is a false expectation, so let me dispel it right now. It comes from our conditioning in having a nine-to-five job where we get a pay packet each week. Remember that share trading is a business and therefore there is no guarantee of a regular income. Like many other businesses, share trading can be very cyclical in nature. Of course, just how cyclical depends largely on how we go about it.

But before we delve into the science of share trading, we need to look at some of the general issues associated with running a share trading business. So now I'm going to switch from share trader to business consultant to help you get ready to start trading shares.

Get ready to trade

I know this is going to sound like very basic stuff to anyone who is already in business, but it is a necessary part of the overall process of becoming a share trader. Just like in any other type of business, you need to do your ground work, and this will also help to give you the right psychological cues to understand that what you're developing is a business and not just a hobby. Here are some of the key things you need to do to get started:

- Register a business name and/or set up appropriate financial structure(s).
- Set up a bank account and find yourself a broker (full service or online).
- Have a dedicated work space and a set timetable for when you trade.
- Establish a business plan with goals and timelines. Include your share trading education.
- Create a review process where you analyse your results and update your strategy(s).

I do not want to drill down into too much detail here because issues such as 'What constitutes an appropriate financial structure?' are obviously beyond the scope of this book. But I will give you a bit of a hand with what is required in the review process. This is a fairly mechanical procedure so I have included a 'Trading performance and strategy review' template at the end of the book (see appendix C). I don't recommend that you even bother looking at it at this point because much of it is related to material in this book that you are yet to read. And there is nothing more dangerous for a share trader than to become distracted. Speaking of which, I strongly recommend that you stick with trading shares and do not try to become an 'everything' trader, as many people are wont to do.

Share traders trade shares

Once you are up and running as a trader, it's very easy to get distracted by all the different financial products and markets, whizzbang software with its bells and whistles, and of course the promises of great wealth. Just the sheer number of books you can buy on trading financial markets can cause no end of confusion. In a way I was lucky when I started trading because all these distractions simply didn't exist and finding even one book on trading was a quest.

A skill universal among successful traders is the ability to read charts. Reading charts, or 'charting', is also known as technical analysis and if you intend trading any type of financial market or product on a relatively short-term basis, technical analysis is an essential skill to have. Given that technical analysis is a prerequisite to understanding most of the material in this book, we examine it more closely in chapter 2.

Chapter 2

What is charting?

The strategies described in this book are based on the short-term behaviour of shares. Price movement is therefore everything, and factors that affect share prices over the longer term are largely irrelevant. We will therefore not concern ourselves with a lengthy explanation of fundamental analysis, nor delve into the esoteric world of macroeconomics.

But rest assured that there's plenty of ground to cover when it comes to technical analysis, which is known as charting. In fact, there's so much material that my first book, *Charting in a Nutshell*, was entirely dedicated to this subject. Thankfully I won't need to be quite as comprehensive in my explanation of charting on this occasion.

You can rely on price

A key point worth mentioning before we start tackling the nitty gritty of this subject is that one of the few totally reliable forms of information to be found in the stock market is historical price activity. Put simply, price charts are based on fact, whereas the financial information relating to companies is open to varying degrees of manipulation. Companies report their own financial numbers and it is rarely in their interest to put out negative information, so they are clearly biased.

An example of this is where a company may be paying a very attractive dividend to its investors, but in fact it could be borrowing money to meet this obligation. This sounds silly given that dividend payments are the mechanism by which companies distribute their profits to their shareholders, but it is not an uncommon occurrence. Several very well known Australian blue chip companies engaged in this practice in recent times.

These companies claim that it is a way to even out investor returns over a period of several years or more, but it is a deceptive practice in my opinion, regardless of the underlying intention(s). It makes the assessment of a company's profitability via its dividend payments a rather dubious practice. And this is just one obvious example of the potentially misleading nature of fundamental analysis.

Another more blatant example is where company directors deliberately set about misleading the marketplace with totally spurious financial reporting. The 2001 collapse of HIH Insurance Ltd, Australia's largest ever corporate failure (at the time of writing), came as a complete surprise to the marketplace. Several of HIH's directors colluded in the false reporting of the company's asset backing and profitability.

This of course is not a common occurrence, but it does demonstrate that a company's reported financials are not always hard and fast facts. Although HIH published false and misleading information, the share price suggested that something was well and truly amiss long before any deception had been uncovered (see figure 2.1). Of course, historical price information cannot be misreported by company directors, or anyone else with a biased interest.

Please don't read too much into my criticism of fundamental analysis because I use it myself, in conjunction with other confirming factors; however, you should maintain a healthy degree of scepticism when employing it. On the other hand, there is an honesty about the prices at which shares trade and this data is reported by the Australian Securities Exchange (ASX) and not the companies themselves.

Figure 2.1: despite its supposedly sound fundamentals, HIH's share price consistently fell in the lead up to its demise.

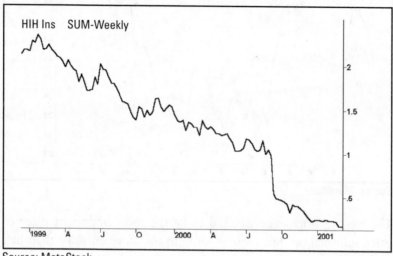

Source: MetaStock

The price information that charts are based on is of a factual nature; however, the interpretation of this information requires the use of discretion. Charting or technical analysis is therefore often considered to be an art as much as a science.

Price versus time

When we are looking at a price chart we are looking at the change in price over a given period of time. The vertical scale on any price chart is the price of the instrument in question, while the horizontal scale is time. The chart in figure 2.2 (overleaf) of BHP Billiton (BHP), showing slightly over 12 months of weekly price activity, is a typical example of the sort of chart you would see in a newspaper or magazine and is the simplest form of price chart. This chart would technically be referred to as a weekly line-on-close chart. A line-on-close chart is created by drawing a line connecting the weekly closing prices of BHP during the period shown.

Figure 2.2: line-on-close weekly price chart of BHP Billiton

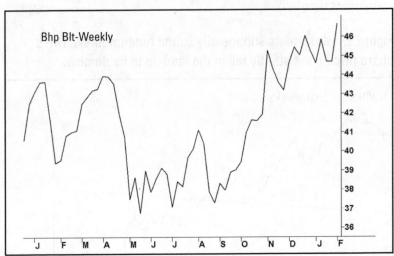

Source: MetaStock

The closing price is considered to be the most important piece of price information, but there is more to the story on price than just the closing price. There are four bits of price information:

- open—the price the market trades at when it first opens
- high—the highest price the market trades at during the trading period
- low—the lowest price the market trades at during the trading period
- close—the last price the market trades at just before the market closes.

In the above explanation and in this context I am using the term 'market' in its generic form. I may describe the buying and selling of any individual share or financial instrument, such as BHP, as a 'market', or I may use it to describe the stock market as a whole. Whichever the case, it should be reasonably obvious what I mean by market from the context in which I am applying it.

Furthermore, as a form of shorthand, I may identify a specific share, such as BHP, by just its share code and not its full name. The share code is the code issued by the ASX to identify that share. Usually,

I will use the company's full name initially, but then refer to it by its share code from that point on.

Let us return to our discussion on price charts.

OHLC bar charts

OHLC is short for open, high, low and close. Probably the simplest way in which to display all four bits of price information is with the aid of the OHLC bar chart (see figure 2.3).

Figure 2.3: typical OHLC bar chart where each bar represents a single trading period

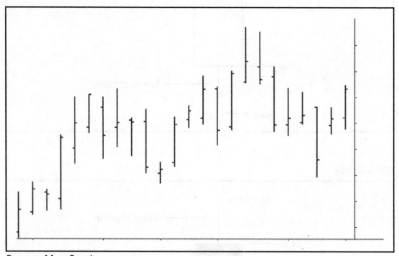

Source: MetaStock

In figure 2.3, each trading period is represented by a bar that has a tick to the left of the bar and another tick to the right. The top of the bar and the bottom of the bar represent the price range of a given trading period (the high and the low), while the tick to the left of the bar is the opening price and the tick to the right represents the closing price.

Candlestick charts

The candlestick chart (see figure 2.4, overleaf) is my personal favourite. It also conveys all four bits of price information. While it is the type of chart that I will be using most in this book, you will also see the other chart types from time to time. Hopefully, this will help you to familiarise yourself with these different types of price charts.

Figure 2.4: types of candlestick charts

White candle

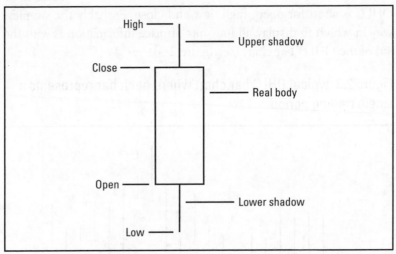

Black candle

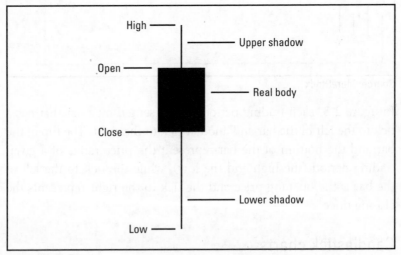

Candlestick charts are a little more complex than the chart types that we have looked at so far and therefore they warrant a slightly more detailed explanation. Candlestick charts use a single candle for each trading period and I personally find them very easy to interpret. The larger section of each candle is called the real body, and the thin parts on the top and bottom are called shadows. A white candle is an up candle, where the close is higher than the open. A black candle is a down candle, where the close is lower than the open.

Candlestick charts originated in Japan and have been in use for several centuries. There is a vast body of material on how to interpret these charts, including a wide variety of names for the different types of candles. To keep this discussion as simple as possible, at this stage there is only one special type of candle that I want to introduce to you—the Doji candle (see figure 2.5).

Figure 2.5: the Doji candle

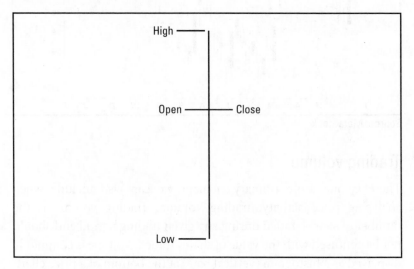

The open and close of the Doji candle are the same, so it doesn't have a real body. As you will see, this lack of trading range between the opening and closing prices has a special significance that we will look into in greater depth later on. In fact, one of the key reasons I am such a fan of candlestick charts is because they visually emphasise the trading range between the opening and closing prices, and this part of the price activity is of major significance.

Let us revisit our 12-month chart of BHP, but this time we'll use candlesticks (see figure 2.6). Compare this chart to the earlier 12-month chart of BHP (see figure 2.2 on p. 18) and you can see how it conveys far more information. Note how the rising price activity is made up of mainly white candles, while the down trends are dominated by black candles.

Figure 2.6: candlestick chart of BHP Billiton

Source: MetaStock

Trading volume

There is one more primary element we can also include when analysing price activity: trading volume. Trading volume is the number of shares traded during any given trading period and should not be confused with the value of shares traded. Volume is commonly displayed as a histogram (vertical bars) at the bottom of a price chart. Adding volume into our chart of BHP gives us the following picture (see figure 2.7), which conveys five discrete bits of information for each trading period.

To work out the number of BHP shares traded in the following chart you need to use a multiplying factor of 100. This is a peculiarity of my charting program, but you will find that most charting programs use a similar approach to keep the numbers on the vertical scale manageable. It should also be noted that the actual number of shares traded is of less importance than the direction in which the volume is trending. I elaborate on this point when we look at breakout trading in part III.

Figure 2.7: candlestick chart of BHP Billiton including volume histogram

Source: MetaStock

Time frame

The last key aspect of the basic price chart that we need to consider is the time frame that you wish to operate in. Until now I have often used the generic term 'trading period' as opposed to a specific period such as daily, weekly or monthly. In the previous charts of BHP, each trading period (or candlestick) is one week, making all of these weekly charts of BHP. If we were to use these weekly charts of BHP, we are performing weekly analysis of BHP.

Once again, this sounds ridiculously simple, but it is extremely important that traders are absolutely clear on what trading period they're using, which is largely determined by the time frame they are working in. The trading strategies outlined in this book are short term (three weeks to three months). Given this time frame, I typically employ weekly analysis coupled with daily execution.

I analyse weekly charts showing at least six months of price activity. When I've determined whether to buy or sell, I normally enter and/ or exit the market on a day-by-day basis. There is no set definition on what is short term, medium term or long term, but every trader needs to be absolutely clear on what time frame they are working in, regardless of what they choose to call it. Here are the definitions that I use, which you may want to adopt:

- very short term: three days to three weeks; daily analysis + daily execution

- short term: three weeks to three months; weekly analysis + daily/weekly execution

- medium term: approx. six months; weekly analysis + daily/weekly execution

- long term: 12 months or more; weekly analysis + weekly execution.

The idea behind share trading for me is *not* to work too hard, and therefore I have little desire to trade in the very short-term time frame, where I have to perform daily analysis. Of course, this is my choice and there are plenty of traders who do operate in this time frame and do so very successfully. On the other hand, trading over a period of 12 months or more is a little too blunt even for my taste and carries an increased exposure to volatility given how rapidly market conditions can change, driven by the shorter and shorter periods of the modern business cycle.

Furthermore, some more experienced traders may accuse me of leaving out 'intraday trading'. But rest assured that this is not an accidental oversight. I have only once met someone who can trade successfully on a consistent basis in this time frame and therefore I don't consider it to be a viable option, particularly because that one individual has such a unique psychological profile that it would be impossible to emulate what he does anyway.

While the idea of sitting down at my computer and generating profits by the hour has great appeal, I would suggest that it is even less realistic than a trader wanting to take profits from the market week in and week out. I therefore do not entertain the intraday time frame and I recommend that you overlook it as well, particularly if you are a novice trader. I suggest that we stay with what is realistic and what best suits our objective of being lazy: short-term time frame with daily or weekly execution.

Now that we've covered the fundamental elements needed to create a price chart, we can delve a bit deeper and look at the array of analysis techniques that we are going to employ in the strategies described in this book. The remainder of this chapter looks at how to use trend lines, while the next chapter covers the more sophisticated concepts and indicators that belong to the modern era of technical analysis.

Trend lines

The simplest indicator and one that should never be underestimated is the humble trend line.

When analysing either an upward or downward trend it is common to use trend lines. A trend line is simply a straight line placed strategically on a chart. In an upward trend, a trend line is constructed by drawing a line that touches two or more of the most significant lows (see figure 2.8, overleaf). These lows are usually the lowest part of the real bodies of the relevant candles, so the lower shadows are usually ignored. The more often the price activity touches the trend line, the more significant the trend. This line provides support to the price action (that is, the price will usually bounce off or stay above this line while the trend is valid) and, when broken by the price activity, indicates that the trend is weakening or may be over.

In a downward trend, a trend line is constructed by drawing a line that touches two or more of the most significant highs (see figure 2.9, overleaf). In this instance, the upper shadows are ignored and the highs are commonly based on the real bodies of the relevant candles. In this case, the downward trend line provides resistance to the price activity; that is, the line provides a ceiling on the price activity while the trend is valid.

Figure 2.8: upward trend line touching the price activity at three separate points

Source: MetaStock

Figure 2.9: downward trend line touching the price activity at three separate points

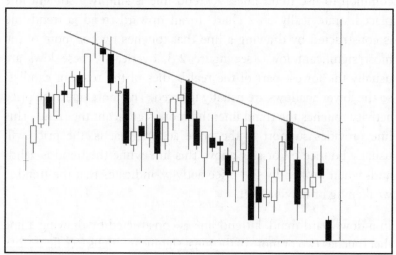

Source: MetaStock

Chartists were using trend lines long before computers existed. Drawing charts by hand was a slow and tedious task. Trend lines were relatively easy to create with a ruler or similar device, so trend lines are one of the oldest and simplest types of analytical tools.

Triangles

As well as defining trends, trend lines can also be used to define other price patterns, such as triangles. While I do not want to explore the behavioural significance of identifying triangles (or consolidation patterns) in great detail at this stage, it is a very important part of my breakout trading strategy and therefore we will closely examine their construction here. As with identifying trends, the shadows of the candles are usually overlooked and the trend line is placed against the real body of the relevant candlesticks (see figure 2.10).

Figure 2.10: triangle or consolidation pattern defined using two converging trend lines

Source: MetaStock

I say that the shadows are *usually* overlooked because this may not always be the case, such as in the example of a triangle pattern shown in figure 2.11 (overleaf).

So it should be noted that the only hard and fast rule is that when using trend lines to define triangular patterns, it is essential that the converging lines capture all of the real bodies of the candlesticks. A chartist may therefore choose to include the shadows or to ignore them. You can now start to appreciate how technical analysis or charting requires the use of discretion.

Figure 2.11: triangle defined using candlestick shadows as well as their real bodies

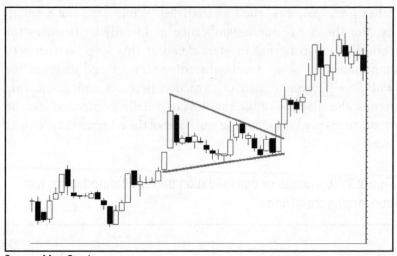

Source: MetaStock

Now we've covered the basics we need to take this subject to the next level by looking at some of the more modern developments in technical analysis: computer-generated indicators. While I've limited the content to only the concepts and indicators relevant to my trading strategies, it still makes for a comprehensive explanation.

Chapter 3

Modern technical analysis

Prior to the advent of personal computers, charting was a manual and fairly tedious pursuit, so analysis techniques rarely went beyond the application of a few trend lines. However, thanks to the introduction of PCs and charting software, we can now generate price charts in a matter of seconds. Moreover, we can very quickly and easily make fairly complex calculations based on price information to design and create a vast range of what we call technical indicators.

In this chapter we extend our previous discussion on charting by focusing on the modern era of technical analysis, where computer-generated charts and technical indicators are the norm. This discussion starts with the most basic building block of most modern technical indicators, the moving average.

Moving averages

One way in which discretion (acting according to one's own judgement) can be minimised is by defining price trends using what chartists call moving averages, as opposed to the manual placement of trend lines. Furthermore, because price activity doesn't always progress in a straight line, it is often more helpful to use moving averages, which 'bend' in sympathy with price activity (see figure 3.1, overleaf).

Figure 3.1: a moving average being used as a trend line

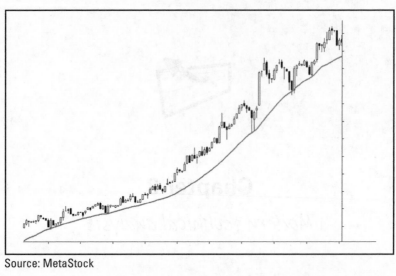

Source: MetaStock

When calculating a moving average it is the convention to use the closing price because it is considered to be the most significant price component. All commercially available charting programs will, by default, use the closing price to calculate moving averages.

Simple moving average

A simple moving average (SMA) smooths out the price activity on a chart by adding together the prices of 'X' number of trading periods and then dividing it by 'X'. As each new trading period occurs, the average is recalculated and all the averages are then connected using a single unbroken line. So to calculate a simple five-week moving average the following formula is applied:

5-week SMA
$$= \frac{\text{Price for week 1 + week 2 + week 3 + week 4 + week 5}}{5}$$

The term 'simple moving average' is used because it is created using the formula for calculating a simple average. This type of moving average has been used by chartists since the early 1900s, although you can appreciate how time-consuming it was to calculate and draw an SMA by hand. Luckily, we have charting software that does it all for us, so creating the following charts (see figures 3.2 and 3.3) took me less than two minutes. Also note that in figure 3.2 (and subsequent charts) I have made the price candlesticks grey so the five-week simple moving average line is easy to see.

Figure 3.2: weekly price chart with a five-week simple moving average (each candle represents one week)

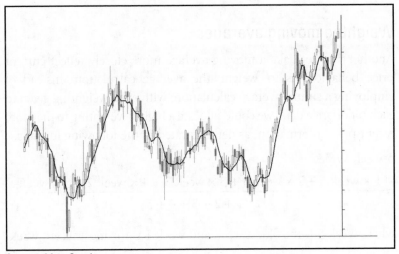

Source: MetaStock

Figure 3.3: five-week SMA (black line) and 20-week SMA (grey line)

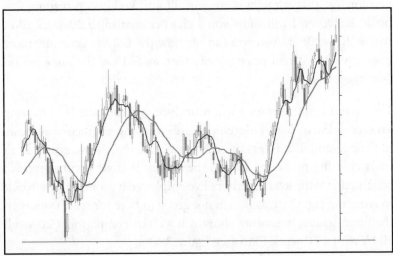

Source: MetaStock

The number of trading periods used to calculate a moving average is entirely up to the chartist and once again we see discretion creeping into the process. However, it should be noted that the lower the number of periods used, the closer the moving average will track the underlying price activity. For instance, in figure 3.3 I've applied both a five-week and a 20-week simple moving average. Note how the five-week SMA travels along much closer to the price activity.

Weighted moving averages

Another way to make a moving average more closely reflect current price behaviour is to 'weight' the average calculation. Instead of employing a simple average calculation, with even weighting given to each bit of price data, we could allocate a higher weighting to the more recent price information, as demonstrated in the following formula:

5-week WMA

$$= \frac{1 \times \text{week } 5 + 2 \times \text{week } 4 + 3 \times \text{week } 3 + 4 \times \text{week } 2 + 5 \times \text{week } 1}{1 + 2 + 3 + 4 + 5}$$

where week 5 is the oldest week and week 1 is the most recent week.

There are different types of weighted moving averages (WMAs), but the most popular one is the exponential moving average (EMA). It employs a formula so complex that I'm not going to show it to you for fear that it might scare you off and you'll stop reading this book. However, I will show you a chart comparing a 20-week EMA with a 20-week SMA so you can see how the EMA is generally more responsive to current price activity than an SMA of the same period (see figure 3.4).

The final moving average I will introduce you to is the Hull moving average (HMA). Yes, I developed this moving average that bears my name and I am very proud to say that it is now available in most charting programs around the world. It is yet another type of weighted moving average where I've employed a geometric approach to reducing lag. Once again I'm not going to bore (or scare) you with the finer details, but rather show you a chart comparing a 20-week HMA with a 20-week EMA (see figure 3.5).

Figure 3.4: 20-week EMA (black line) and 20-week SMA (grey line)

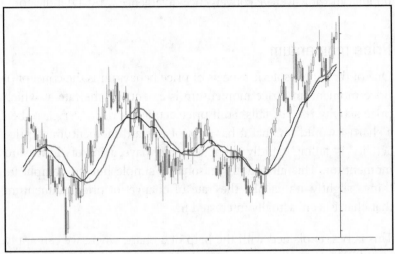

Source: MetaStock

Figure 3.5: 20-week HMA (black line) and 20-week EMA (grey line)

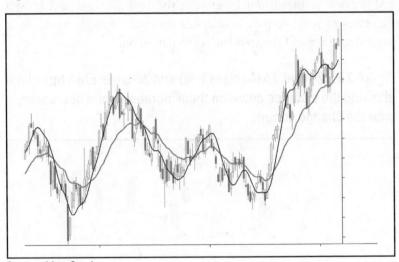

Source: MetaStock

The HMA is the winner when it comes to reducing price lag because it more closely tracks the price activity and therefore it is the most ideal moving average for capturing the underlying price trend. Hence, it is the logical choice for forming the basis of some of the more sophisticated indicators that we'll be employing later on in this book. Now we need to go back to the exponential moving average as we embark on an explanation of price momentum and the very popular moving average convergence divergence (MACD) indicator.

Price momentum

One of the more esoteric aspects of price behaviour is the concept of price momentum. Price momentum is essentially the rate at which price activity rises or falls. So if price activity is rising very fast then a chartist would say that it has a lot of upward momentum. If price activity is falling rapidly then it would have a lot of downward momentum. This all sounds reasonably simple but, to complicate things slightly, it's usually the 'rate of change' of price momentum that chartists are actually interested in.

This is best explained with the help of a chart, where we can apply two different moving averages and observe how they interact with each other. In figure 3.6 I've applied both a 12-week and a 26-week EMA. Look at the distance between the two averages and how it increases as price activity accelerates upwards, then decreases as it begins to falter and the trend starts to flatten out.

Figure 3.6: 12-week EMA (black line) and 26-week EMA (grey line) showing the distance between them increasing and decreasing with the change in trend

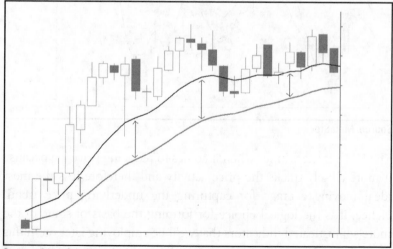

Source: MetaStock

This distance is directly related to the gradient of the trend and is therefore a representation of price momentum. As this distance increases, the momentum is increasing, and when it decreases, momentum is decreasing. We're primarily interested in the change in momentum, so the actual distance being measured is of little significance, whereas the 'change' in this distance is very important.

Of course, the distance between these two lines can be easily worked out by simply subtracting one from the other. This is done by subtracting the 26-period EMA (the slower of the two moving averages) from the 12-period EMA (the faster moving average). We can then display this value as a line in what we call a subchart or subwindow at either the top or the bottom of the price chart. This value will vary along with any change in price trend and will allow us to easily observe the change in momentum. Figure 3.7 shows both the 12-week and 26-week EMAs, as well as the difference between them, in a subchart above the price chart.

Figure 3.7: the line at the top is the difference between the 12-week EMA (black line) and 26-week EMA (grey line)

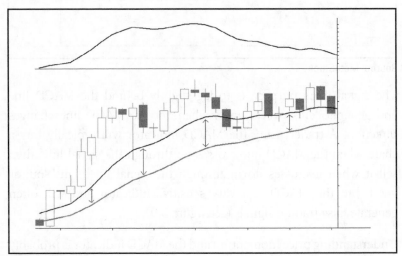

Source: MetaStock

The MACD indicator

Readers with a bit of experience in technical analysis will know that what I've been describing is the construction of the moving average convergence divergence (MACD) line. Gerald Appel developed the MACD indicator in the 1960s. The MACD indicator consists of two lines: the MACD line and a signal line, which is a nine period EMA of the MACD line (the signal line is referred to in some texts and charting programs as a reference or trigger line). Figure 3.8 is an example of a MACD line and signal line.

Figure 3.8: MACD indicator at the top with the MACD line (black) and the signal line (grey)

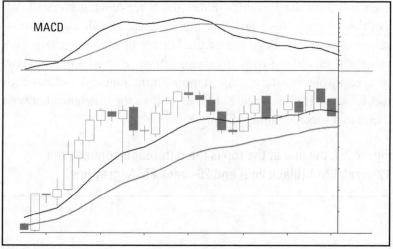

Source: MetaStock

The signal line's purpose is to lag slightly behind the MACD line and generate 'crossover' signals whenever the MACD line changes direction. A trader using the MACD indicator will typically buy a share when the MACD line crosses up through the signal line, then sell it when it crosses down through the signal line. This sounds good, but the MACD is a very sensitive indicator and will often generate false trading signals (see figure 3.9).

Understanding price momentum and the MACD indicator is probably as hard as it gets, technically speaking. I show you a very reliable and robust technique for employing the MACD indicator to generate momentum-based exit signals in my breakout trading strategy.

We have just one more topic we need to cover: volatility.

Figure 3.9: MACD indicator giving false trading signals while price activity continues to trend up

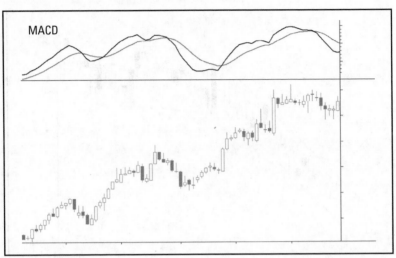

Source: MetaStock

Volatility

Price volatility is the degree of instability of price activity over time. Putting it another way, volatility is the measurement of how much price activity deviates over a given period. An explanation with charts is probably the best way of getting this concept across, so have a look at figure 3.10 (overleaf), where instead of observing the overall trend as we have been doing previously, we are now interested in the very short-term price oscillations. To help you visualise this, I've used some trend lines to create price channels.

Price volatility is the width of these channels and you can see how the price channel tends to be fairly narrow when price activity is trending, but widens as the price activity starts to flatten out and trade sideways. Volatility is therefore relatively low when the market is trending, but tends to increase as the trend diminishes. This linkage between the trending behaviour of price activity and its underlying volatility is often exploited by chartists to give early warning of a change in trend direction. One important point to note is that volatility is unrelated to the 'direction' of price movement and is therefore a measurement of magnitude only.

Figure 3.10: channels highlighting the trading range of price activity when trending upwards and sideways

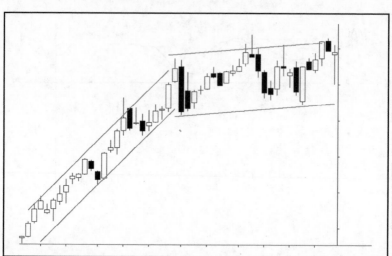

Source: MetaStock

Volatility is widely employed in stop loss indicators, which are used by traders to decide when to exit trades. But to do this, we obviously require some way of quantitatively analysing volatility. We need to look at how we can measure volatility. While there are many ways to quantify price deviation, for our purposes we will limit this discussion to just two methods: average true range and multiple moving averages.

Average true range

The first technique we'll look at is a measurement known as true range, which was developed by J Welles Wilder, an American engineer and stock trader. Wilder wanted to develop a way to determine how much the price of any given financial instrument varied during the most recent trading period. To do this he had to include the closing price from the previous trading period as a point of reference. What's more, he only wanted to know the maximum trading range; therefore, he defined true range as being the largest of the following three measurements:

1   the difference between the current high and the current low

2   the difference between the current high and the previous close

3   the difference between the current low and the previous close.

These measurements are far easier to visualise with a diagram (see figure 3.11).

Figure 3.11: measurements used to define true range

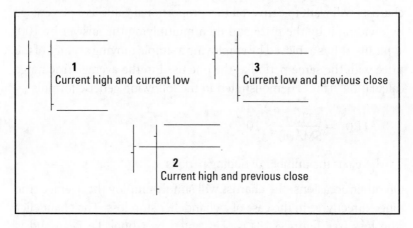

Average true range is the average of all the true range measurements taken over a given period. Figure 3.12 is a price chart with its 15-week average true range, or ATR(15), shown in the subwindow below the price chart.

Figure 3.12: the ATR(15) indicates increased volatility as the trend flattens out

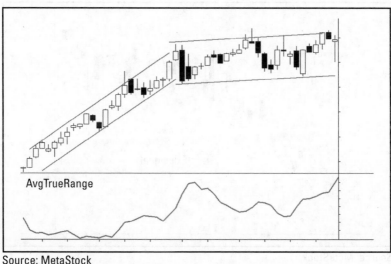

Source: MetaStock

Once again, we see discretion come into the process as each chartist/ trader must determine over which period he or she wishes to observe volatility. Note that average true range returns an absolute value that is directly linked to the underlying price activity. So for some purposes chartists will want to convert it to a proportional value as a percentage by dividing it by the price and then multiplying the answer by 100. Typically, this is achieved by employing a simple moving average of the price with the same period as the one used in the average true range calculation. This is demonstrated in the following generic formula:

$$\%\mathrm{ATR}(n) = \frac{\mathrm{ATR}(n)}{\mathrm{SMA}(n)} \times 100$$

where n is the number of trading periods

On other occasions, the chartist will simply employ the average true range directly, as in the case of a chandelier stop loss. The chandelier stop loss (see figure 3.13) was invented by Chuck Le Beau and is constructed by subtracting a multiple of the average true range value from the most recent high in a rising trend. This chart shows a chandelier stop loss that is created using an ATR period of 15 and a multiplier of 2; that is, the most recent high $- 2 \times \mathrm{ATR}(15)$.

Figure 3.13: the grey line is a chandelier stop loss employing ATR(15) and a multiplier of 2

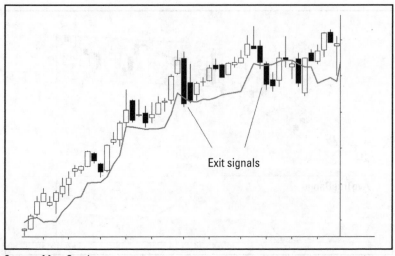

Exit signals

Source: MetaStock

Being able to measure price volatility serves an important and useful purpose, and average true range is a relatively quick and simple way to go about it, but it is by no means the only way of measuring price volatility. Now we're going to look at how volatility can be assessed from a qualitative perspective and used for a purpose other than determining when to sell.

Multiple moving averages

So far we've looked at how volatility can be used to generate exit signals. Now I want to look at another technique for measuring volatility and one that will help us decide whether or not to actually enter a trade. Multiple moving averages (MMAs) are a fairly modern development in technical analysis and that's because you certainly wouldn't want to have to draw them by hand.

MMAs are a series of moving averages all drawn on the same chart with different but usually evenly spaced periods. When creating an MMA chart, it is common practice to hide the underlying financial instrument, as I have done in figure 3.14, where the actual price activity isn't displayed and it only shows the MMAs.

Figure 3.14: MMA chart created using 10 evenly spaced periods

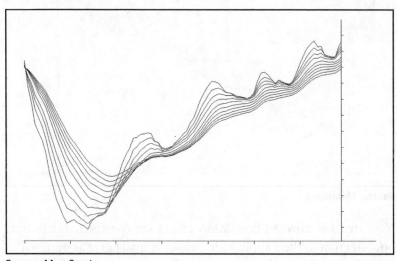

Source: MetaStock

Placing a series of moving averages on the same chart with evenly spaced period values forms a ribbon that filters out the short-term price movements, but highlights the underlying trend. This technique was adopted several decades ago by Daryl Guppy, an internationally renowned share trader and best-selling author, who came up with the idea of splitting the ribbon into two distinct groups.

The shorter term group of averages represents the shorter term traders in the market, while the longer term group represents the more conservative, longer term traders and investors. Daryl prefers using EMAs and employs MMA charts in a variety of different ways, but principally for trend analysis. However, the one way Daryl and I differ is that he trades with daily charts while I use weekly charts. Because of this, we invariably use different periods. On a weekly basis I recommend using 3, 5, 7, 9, 11, 13, 21, 24, 27, 30, 33 and 36 weeks. Figure 3.15 is an example of a weekly MMA chart.

Figure 3.15: weekly MMA chart created using EMAs, with the shorter term group in grey and the longer term group in black

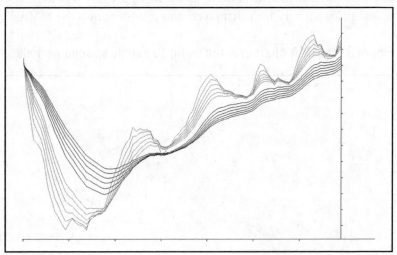

Source: MetaStock

Now that I've covered how MMA charts are constructed, let's turn our attention to their application, which is qualitative as opposed to quantitative. Essentially, I use MMA charts to judge the quality of a trend, my principle concern being the degree of volatility in the price behaviour. Let's start by looking at an ideal trend where there is a little bit of short-term volatility, but all the long term group of lines on the chart are remaining relatively straight, evenly spread out and parallel to each other (see figure 3.16).

Figure 3.16: MMA chart showing an ideal trend with very low volatility

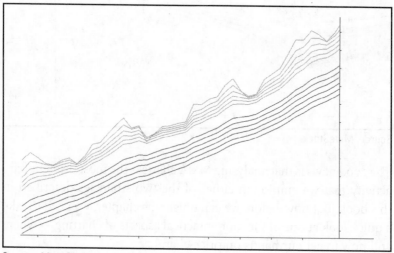

Source: MetaStock

Looking at the short-term group of averages, you can see how the market runs and then pulls back, over and over again. This is normal trending behaviour as markets repeatedly rally, then rest. But it should be an even and regular pattern that isn't too violent. If it is very aggressive, it indicates that the very short-term traders have a strong influence over the market and, as a result, the trend is inherently unstable. Let's look at this type of situation (see figure 3.17, overleaf), where the price activity has far too much short-term volatility and would therefore be considered unstable.

I would buy into the ideal trend but not into the unstable one because it is far less likely to survive, in my opinion. And there's the kicker—it is only my opinion. Analysing MMA charts is entirely discretionary and requires a considerable amount of practice if you want to do it well. Hence, MMA chart interpretation is more akin to an art than a science.

Figure 3.17: MMA chart showing an unstable trend

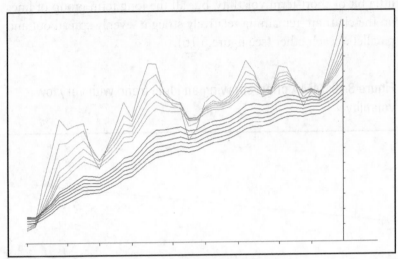

Source: MetaStock

The good news is that analysing MMA charts is the most discretionary activity that we employ in either of the two strategies described in this book. But now, before we can finish this chapter, we need to take a quick look at one of the more practical aspects of charting—where and how to get our hands on price charts.

Access to price charts

To be a chartist you must have access to price charts; fortunately, there are a number of ways you can access them. The first one is the most obvious and cheapest method and that is to simply do an internet search for 'free ASX charts' or something similar. This will return a number of choices and you probably won't know where to start. However, it isn't what I'd do.

Free online software is usually very basic and it is put out for free in the hope that you'll trial it and then upgrade to the full commercial version anyway. The integrity of the market data being used is simply unknown and while I can't say it's good or bad, I suggest that making trading decisions based on this market data is a somewhat dubious practice. In short, when it comes to charting software, you get what you pay for, regardless of all the hype on the internet.

The bottom line is this: if you're serious about trading, you should use the proper tools for the job, and that means spending money. A decent charting program will set you back about $1000 and end-of-day ASX market data will cost around $500 per annum. I recommend:

- Educated Investor Financial Bookshop for charting software <www.educatedinvestor.com.au>

- Justdata for end-of-day ASX market data <www.justdata.com. au>.

The alternative to buying your own charting software and getting your head around it is to subscribe to my newsletter services. I discuss these further when we start looking at my two trading systems.

This is a fairly rudimentary introduction to charting, but it is necessary to understand for the purpose of reading and comprehending the rest of this book. However, a much more detailed explanation can be gleaned from my book *Charting in a Nutshell, 2nd edition*. Now let's turn our attention to the most important aspect of successful share trading—how to manage risk.

Chapter 4

Risk management

I'm about to give you the succinct 'how to' version on risk management, but before I get down to the nuts and bolts of how to avoid blowing yourself up, let me make one thing absolutely clear:

Sound risk management is a mandatory requirement for successful share trading.

I could enter into a long, wordy introduction on what risk management is all about, but it will serve little purpose other than to chase off a lot of readers—so I won't. Furthermore, most texts on this subject are what one would call decidedly dry (read: long and boring), so I'll attempt to keep this discussion mildly amusing and moving along as quickly as possible.

In this chapter we'll look at:

- expectancy—the financial viability of your trading strategy
- money management—managing your losses
- catastrophic risk—the possibility of an unexpected event
- capital allocation—spreading your capital across different risk segments.

Consider these topics to be the peas, carrots and broccoli of share trading: an essential part of your diet if you want to grow up to be a big, strong and healthy share trader.

Expectancy

I'm yet to meet anyone who would knowingly employ a trading strategy that will lose money over time, but there are certainly plenty of traders who do exactly that. The reason for this is simple: they're not constantly assessing their trading performance (or don't know how to) and are therefore unaware that their system actually has a negative expectation. It's a bit like slowly cooking a frog so it's blissfully unaware of its impending doom.

To avoid this trap, during our regular trading review (as discussed in chapter 1) we need to measure our expectancy. Expectancy is the average return that a trader can expect from each trade they enter, based on a combination of the win:lose ratio and reward:loss ratio of their trading system. It is a test of a trading system's viability and the first step in risk management. It's also best explained with the help of a working example, so let's take a look at the humble game of coin toss.

Tossing a coin

When tossing a coin it's reasonable to expect that the number of wins will equal the number of losses. Put another way, the probability of winning is 50 per cent. Normally, this simple game of chance is played with an even wager where the benefit of winning is identical to the cost of losing; that is, you receive $1 for a win and pay out $1 for a loss. Now let's plug these numbers into the formula for calculating expectancy:

$$\text{Expectancy} = (\text{probability of winning} \times \text{avg win/avg loss}) - \text{probability of losing}$$

Transposing our numbers for the game of coin toss we get:

$$\text{Expectancy} = (0.5 \times \$1/\$1) - 0.5 = \text{zero}$$

Note how I have converted the probability of winning and losing to a decimal fraction, so a probability of 50 per cent is expressed as 0.5 in the formula. Thus, the humble game of coin toss is a fair one as the average expected return on each $1 wagered is zero or neutral—no gain and no loss. Now let's play with the numbers a little by assuming that you will receive $2 for every win, but you still only have to pay out $1 each time you lose:

Expectancy = (0.5 × $2/$1) – 0.5 = 0.5 or 50 per cent

In this instance, for every $1 wagered, on average you can expect a return of 50 per cent. This is a pretty attractive situation and no doubt it's the very reason why no-one will play coin toss with you if you insist on a payout ratio of $2 to $1. But as silly as it seems, many a trader will be on the losing side of the market with a trading system that has a negative expectancy. To illustrate this, let's now take some numbers from a hypothetical trading system where the expectancy is negative and the trader is ultimately doomed:

- number of winning trades = 30
- number of losing trades = 20
- average size of win = $1900
- average size of loss = $3000.

So the trader is winning 30 out of 50 trades, or 60 per cent of the time, and losing 20 out of 50 trades, or 40 per cent of the time:

Expectancy = (0.6 × $1900/$3000) – 0.4 = –0.02 or –2 per cent

In this example the trading system is actually winning most of the time, but the losses outweigh the wins by such a large amount that the net result is an expected average loss of 2 per cent per trade. In other words, don't do it. Now to an example with a positive expectancy:

- number of winning trades = 27
- number of losing trades = 33
- average size of win = $1800
- average size of loss = $1000.

So the trader is winning 27 out of 60 trades, or 45 per cent of the time, and losing 33 out of 60 trades, or 55 per cent of the time:

Expectancy = (0.45 × $1800/$1000) – 0.55 = 0.26 or 26 per cent

This is a far more attractive scenario, where the average return on each trade taken is 26 per cent. Note that most of the trades are actually losing trades.

It's amazing how we are attracted to trading systems that have very high win:lose ratios, but tend to overlook the reward:loss ratio. This is because we humans just love to win and be right—even if it means losing money.

Positive expectancy

I could prattle on about how the higher the expectancy is, the better, then give you a long list of ways to optimise your expectancy, but frankly the bottom line with expectancy is that it must be positive. If expectancy is negative then don't trade. I start to get a bit concerned if my expectancy gets below 20 per cent. This is like a low oil pressure warning in a car—you don't have to immediately stop driving, but you do need to keep a close eye on it.

To work out a trading system's expectancy, either use existing results if they're available, or build up a record of at least 30 trades. This is best done by applying your trading system on paper rather than with real money. Historical results are okay, but generating your own results by paper trading in real time is better in my opinion because you will inevitably have greater faith in the system if it has proven itself to you. You need to ascertain the following parameters:

- number of winning trades
- number of losing trades
- average profit of all winning trades
- average loss of all losing trades.

Furthermore, historical results don't mean much if the trading system requires a degree of discretion in its execution because the results are then based on someone else's discretion and not yours. An integral part of my active trading strategy is the interpretation of MMA charts; therefore, any historical results are highly dependent on whoever was driving the trading system. On the other hand, my breakout trading strategy is largely mechanical and therefore the historical results from this system are quite reliable.

So paper trading does serve a purpose and it will do wonders for your confidence if you have done 30 trades and returned a positive expectancy. But let me temper this with a caveat: expectancy reveals the 'average' expected return for each dollar wagered and this doesn't mean that you can expect this return every time.

Furthermore, expectancy is in a constant state of flux because market conditions continue to change over time, which is why it is imperative that we continue to test and measure our trading system's ongoing performance. While we must make sure that our trading system always has a positive expectancy, it is only one aspect of risk management, so now we need to look at the next essential ingredient: how to manage our losses.

Money management

Money management should really be called 'loss management' because that's exactly what it is. Let's go back for a moment to the humble game of coin toss where we know that the outcome of heads versus tails is 50:50. What will happen if I toss a coin 100 times, then graph the balance of outcomes (see figure 4.1)?

Figure 4.1: balance of outcomes for 100 coin tosses

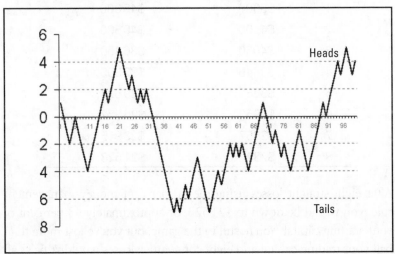

Even though the probability of heads versus tails is 50:50, it doesn't mean that the outcomes will alternate perfectly between heads and tails. In fact, in the previous example, at one point the balance of outcomes is in favour of tails by seven tosses. So even though your trading system has a positive expectancy, it doesn't mean you're immune from a string of losses occurring. In fact, any experienced trader will tell you that a string of up to 10 straight losses isn't all that uncommon. So what can we do about it?

The trick is to limit your losses so you won't blow up while you're patiently waiting for your trading system's positive expectancy to do its thing. This is achieved with the help of a money management rule that tells us how much money we're allowed to put at risk on each trade.

Here's an example of a 10 per cent money management rule where each consecutive loss is 10 per cent of the current total capital. Let's assume that our initial total capital, which is the total amount of money we have available for trading, including both cash on hand and any open positions, is $50 000. So our first loss would be 10 per cent of $50 000, which is $5000, and the second loss would be 10 per cent of $45 000, which is $4500, and so on (see table 4.1).

Table 4.1: 10 per cent money management rule and starting capital of $50 000

Loss	Amount lost	Total capital after loss
1	$5000	$45 000
2	$4500	$40 500
3	$4050	$36 450
4	$3645	$32 805
5	$3281	$29 524
6	$2952	$26 572
7	$2657	$23 915
8	$2392	$21 523

After eight straight losses using the 10 per cent money management rule, you would be down to $21 523, or approximately 43 per cent of your starting capital. You're still in the game, but you've lost more than half your trading capital and eight consecutive losses wouldn't be at all uncommon. The problem here is that a 10 per cent money management rule is far too aggressive and we need to take a much more conservative approach to establishing a workable money management rule.

The 2 per cent risk rule

I now introduce the 2 per cent money management rule, which commonly goes by the shorter name of 'the 2 per cent risk rule'. The equity curves shown in figure 4.2 were created using the 10 per cent risk rule and the 2 per cent risk rule, and illustrate how many losses it takes to reduce $50 000 to $5000 in each case.

Figure 4.2: equity curves created with 10 per cent and 2 per cent risk rules

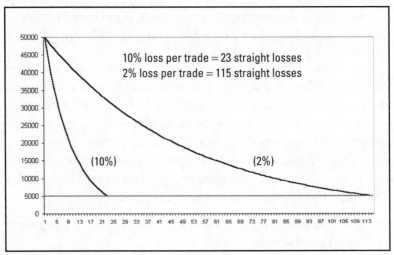

Source: MetaStock

From these results it's fairly clear which risk rule successful traders use. Here it is in an easy-to-remember sentence which it pays to know by heart:

Never risk more than 2 per cent of total capital on any individual trade.

Here's another related saying, but you don't have to know it by heart:

There are old traders and bold traders ... but no old, bold traders.

Of course, if you do actually reach 100 consecutive losses then stop what you're doing, because it's obviously not working. I'll also bet you 10 to 1 that you haven't been monitoring your expectancy.

When we combine these two cornerstones of modern risk management—money management and expectancy—the result is a pretty bulletproof approach to fiscal survival as a share trader. But so far it's all been theory about tossing coins and drawing pretty equity curves. We need to get back to the reality of day-to-day share trading and look at how we actually apply the 2 per cent risk rule.

Using stop losses

When I teach novice traders the 2 per cent risk rule, the most common misconception is that I mean you can allocate only 2 per cent of your total capital to each trade. In other words, if you have $100000 to trade with, you can spend a maximum of only $2000 per trade.

This is wrong because as share traders we use stop losses, and therefore we place only a proportion of the total value of each trade at risk. A stop loss is simply a price point at which we admit that a trade has gone horribly wrong and we're prepared to sell and close out the position (the terms 'trade' and 'position' mean the same thing). We're not risking the entire value of each position and therefore we don't have to limit the size of each trade to 2 per cent of total capital. This is probably best explained with a working example.

- Let's assume our total capital is $100000 and we're using the 2 per cent risk rule.

- We've found a share that is trending up nicely and we can buy it at $5.00 (see figure 4.3).

- Our stop loss strategy is a non-retreating 10 per cent drawdown stop loss, where the stop loss ratchets up every time the market makes a new high, but can't retreat when it falls. Our buy price is therefore $5.00 and our initial stop loss is $4.50, which means if the price drops below this level we will immediately exit the market and cut our losses.

- Our 'loss per share' is therefore $5.00 − $4.50 = 50 cents.

- Using the 2 per cent risk rule, we're prepared to place at risk 2 per cent of $100 000, which is $2000.

- The total number of shares we can buy is therefore $2000/50 cents = 4000 shares.

Figure 4.3: a share that's trending up nicely with a 10 per cent trailing stop loss

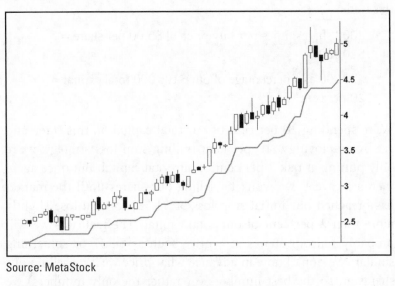

Source: MetaStock

Testing our example, we get the following results:

- if we own 4000 shares and our loss per share is 50 cents, we will lose $2000

- $2000 is 2 per cent of our total capital of $100 000, so our arithmetic is correct.

Position sizing

What we've actually done here is calculate the position size of this trade using the following parameters:

- 2 per cent of our total capital

- our buy price and our initial stop loss price

- our loss per share (that is, our buy price minus the initial stop loss).

The formula to calculate the position size is:

The number of shares we can buy
= 2 per cent of our total capital divided by the loss per share

We'll now go a step further and convert the position size to a percentage of our total capital, which will illustrate the point that we're certainly spending more than 2 per cent of our total capital on this trade:

- 4000 shares times our buy price of $5.00 per share = $20 000

- $20 000 as a percentage of our $100 000 total capital = 20 per cent

We're spending 20 per cent of our total capital on this trade and yet by employing a 10 per cent trailing stop loss strategy, we're only putting at risk 2 per cent of our total capital. But once again there's a caveat: we won't be selling our shares until the market has breached our initial stop loss of $4.50, so we'll lose slightly more than 2 per cent of our total capital. The reality is we will probably sell our shares at a price such as $4.37 or something similar. We don't know in advance what price we'll be selling our shares at, so the best numbers (or rather the only numbers) we have to work with are the ones we know before we enter the trade. Now you can see why we need to take such a conservative approach to managing risk if we want to survive in the real world of share trading.

Trailing stop losses

One other area of confusion for novice traders is the question of why we don't use the initial stop loss price throughout an entire trade. This is because as a trend develops, a trailing stop loss will gradually rise with the trend, ultimately locking in profit. As shown in figure 4.4, we entered the market in the circled area at $5.00, when the 10 per cent drawdown stop loss was $4.50. The trend has continued, however, and the share is now trading at more than $7.00 and the stop loss is $6.35.

Figure 4.4: the trend has continued and the trailing stop loss is now at $6.35

Source: MetaStock

When the stop loss has moved higher than it was at the point of entry, our risk is diminished. When the stop loss becomes greater than our entry price we have effectively locked in profit. The initial stop loss price is used for our position sizing calculations at the start of the trade, but abandoned in favour of a trailing stop loss as the trend develops.

It is imperative that share traders employ some type of trailing stop loss if they hope to lock in profit. Of course, once the stop loss has exceeded the initial entry price, the trade no longer represents any risk and risk management becomes redundant. At this point, a share trader may choose to implement profit-taking strategies, but profit taking isn't a mandatory requirement of successful share trading and so I have excluded it from this discussion. Employing some type of trailing stop loss strategy, however, is a mandatory requirement.

Please re-read this section on money management, stop losses and position sizing as many times as it takes for you to get your head around it. It is vital to your success as a share trader and you simply have to know it before you can safely commence share trading. I do all the position sizing calculations for you in my weekly newsletters; however, it is imperative that you understand and fully appreciate the underlying theory behind these calculations.

What we have been looking at here is position risk where we regulate the size of our losses by adjusting our position size. This is a critical aspect of risk management and goes hand-in-hand with expectancy. We now need to look at the possibility of the totally unexpected happening and what, if anything, we can do about it.

Catastrophic risk

Ensuring your trading system's expectancy is positive and keeping your position risk at around 2 per cent per trade will virtually ensure your success as a share trader—providing the unexpected doesn't happen and blow you up. I've personally witnessed many stock market crashes and company failures over the past several decades and can assure you that the unexpected will most definitely happen at some point.

To ensure our long-term survival as share traders we need to expect the unexpected. The best way for me to deal with the different types of catastrophic risk that you can expect to encounter as a share trader is to simply tackle them one by one, starting with portfolio risk.

Portfolio risk

The most obvious type of catastrophic risk that we face by being in the stock market on a day-by-day basis is the possibility of being caught in a stock market crash. I've never been caught totally unawares in a full-scale crash, but I have been caught in the flow-on effect of a sudden correction in overseas stock markets. The biggest problem with foreign markets is that they trade while we're sleeping and by the time you wake up and discover what's happened, so has everybody else.

If we resign ourselves to the fact that we're going to take a hit to our entire portfolio at some point, we must implement measures that will mitigate the impact of this hit as much as possible. The first preventative measure that we can take is to limit our total market exposure or, putting it more technically, our portfolio risk. Portfolio risk is simply the total of our position risks and is calculated in the following way:

Portfolio risk = position risk × total number of open positions

If we're using the 2 per cent risk rule and we have 10 open positions, our portfolio risk is 20 per cent.

It is our intention to always apply the 2 per cent risk rule, so the only way in which we can regulate our portfolio risk is to control the maximum number of positions we have open at any given time. I recommend that your portfolio risk never exceeds 20 per cent, so the maximum number of positions you can have open at any given time should never be more than 10.

Sector risk

Just as we don't want to be overexposed to the stock market in general, neither do we want to be overexposed to any one particular sector. I'm sure you've heard of the tech boom that came to a crashing halt at the turn of the new millennium. This was a sector-specific catastrophic event and is best illustrated with the help of the US's NASDAQ index, which was, and still is, heavily weighted in favour of technology stocks (see figure 4.5).

Figure 4.5: the NASDAQ index showing the catastrophic end of the tech boom

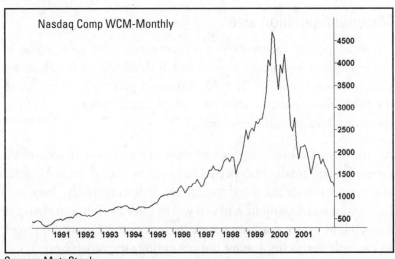

Source: MetaStock

If you think this couldn't happen to us, think again, because it would take several pages to display the charts of all the resource sector corrections that we've had in Australia over the past few decades. Unlike the simple problem of portfolio risk, the issues here are a little more complex because we have to deal with our total capital exposure per sector, as well as our total position risk per sector. We therefore require a two-pronged solution that will address both issues:

- maximum of 40 per cent of total capital per sector
- maximum of three positions per sector.

Based on the assumption that we're employing the 2 per cent risk rule, our total position risk per sector would be 2 per cent times a maximum of three positions, which equals a total position risk per sector of 6 per cent. Note that sector risk is easily subject to fudging because it's not very hard to own stocks outside of one particular sector that are directly related to the fortunes of that sector. For example, rather than own a resource company, a trader may own an engineering firm that supplies only resource sector companies with engineering solutions. Obviously, its fortunes are directly related to the resource sector, so the trader has overexposed themselves to the resource sector while technically not breaching their sector risk rules. A little bit of self honesty is required here because there is an overwhelming urge to pile all of your money into a single outperforming sector. I know—I've done it.

Maximum position size

The last aspect of catastrophic risk management that we're going to tackle is maximum position size, which thankfully is a little more straightforward than sector risk. Maximum position size addresses the problem of specific equity risk, which is the opposite end of the spectrum from general market risk.

All the stop losses in the world won't protect you if something disastrous and totally unexpected happens to one of the companies you own. In such instances the market will most likely drop well below your stop loss figure and you will be forced to sell your shares at a much lower price than you originally anticipated. Figure 4.6 shows an example of this unpleasant but not entirely improbable event.

Figure 4.6: price activity gaps well beyond your stop loss

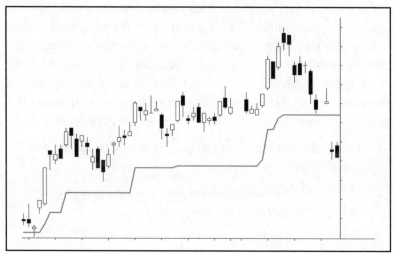

Source: MetaStock

In this situation the 2 per cent risk rule will be of little comfort and our only protection is to limit the absolute maximum amount of capital that we allocate to each position to no more than 20 per cent of our total capital. It's a blunt but effective solution against the unknown happening and has saved my bank account from having a major meltdown on more than one occasion.

We now need to look at the different categories of risk that different types of financial instruments and time frames represent, and what we need to do about it.

Capital allocation

The trading systems included in this book are short term and predominantly cover small to midcap shares, whereas my active investing strategy is designed for trading blue chip shares over a longer time frame. Blue chip shares are the elephants of the stock market, so they experience far less volatility than small to midcap companies. On this basis, blue chip shares are far less likely to give us a nasty surprise, so we can generally categorise blue chip shares as low risk and small to midcap shares as medium risk.

I personally consider any type of derivative trading where significant leverage is being employed as high risk and tend to treat this risk segment as sport rather than a serious part of my overall trading strategy. On this basis, I would only ever contemplate allocating a relatively small amount of my overall capital to this type of trading and certainly no more than 10 per cent of my total capital. We therefore need to spread our capital across these three different risk segments in accordance with the level of risk they represent:

1 60 per cent low risk—my active investing strategy for blue chip shares

2 30 per cent medium risk—my active trading and breakout trading strategies

3 10 per cent high risk—leveraged instruments: CFDs, forex, futures and so on.

You're rarely, if ever, likely to engage in any high risk type of trading activity. If you do, however, I recommend the following capital allocation:

1 67 per cent low risk—my active investing strategy for blue chip shares

2 33 per cent medium risk—my active trading and breakout trading strategies.

The trading strategies presented in this book don't provide a complete trading solution unless they're used in conjunction with a suitable low-risk trading system. Don't underestimate the importance of capital allocation to your long-term survival. Blue chip share trading may be a relatively boring exercise, but it is a successful share trader's bread and butter.

Don't dabble

While this may sound a bit incongruous at this point, don't dabble in the market. If you're going to apply a trading system, do it fully and properly. Many would-be traders think that buying just one or two shares is a good way of testing a trading system, when in fact it's the equivalent of driving a car without letting it out of first gear: it won't work and you'll probably break something. So be fully committed, use sound risk management and enjoy the ride.

The great news now is that we've covered all the basics of share trading and we can start to look at the key components of a successful trading system. The best way to do that is by dissecting a successful trading system to see what makes it tick.

Chapter 5
Anatomy of a trade

Trading is a business. Every good business should be well organised and use a clearly defined set of procedures. Nothing should be left to chance ... well, as little as possible anyway. Share traders, just like all businesspeople, should never wake up in the morning and have to ask themselves what they're going to do today.

McDonald's is a classic example of an extremely well organised business where teenagers make up the bulk of the staff. These same teenagers often won't clean up their bedrooms, but after school they get together and run restaurants that turn over millions of dollars per annum, thanks mainly to the company's clear and concise operating procedures.

The share trader's equivalent to a McDonald's procedures manual is their trading system. While this system can include discretionary aspects, it should clearly define the precise steps that the trader must take to implement his or her trading premise. In fact, after risk management, not having a clearly defined trading strategy is the most common reason why traders fail to succeed; hence the cliché 'failing to plan is planning to fail'.

The key components

We're now going to break down a successful trading system into its component parts so you can see what makes it tick. The really important point here is that virtually every trading system can be broken down into several key (or universal) components. Like driving a car, it helps to have a basic understanding of the major components that make it work, such as the engine, gearbox and drive train. So here are the key components you need for a trading system, starting with the most important component of all—the trading premise:

- Trading premise. If your trading premise is sound then your trading system will inevitably be profitable. Remember the facts about the stock market that I talked about in the preface: share prices tend to trend and share prices cannot remain at rest indefinitely. These observations are the trade premises on which the trading systems described in this book are based. Their success depends on these observations being valid, so the trading premise is the foundation stone of any trading system.

- Search procedure(s). The first stage in most trading systems is to search the market for trading opportunities that meet the requirements of our trade premise. This is the bit most of us really enjoy because it is the hunting phase. It typically involves a series of filters that identify what shares to buy, but can also include more general filters that tell us whether we should be in the market at all. For instance, it's a bit contradictory for a trend trader to be trying to buy rising shares in a falling market. We'll discuss this more as we get down to the nuts and bolts of my active investing strategy.

- Entry trigger or triggers used. When some potential trading opportunities have been identified, it is common practice among traders to further refine the moment of entry by applying an even finer filter to control the specific moment of market entry. I say common practice because employing an entry trigger is not an absolutely essential requirement for a trading system. Mind you, I rarely feel comfortable trading without one.

- Exit criteria (reasons for leaving the market). Trading is about exploiting price movement. A trader must use some type of trailing stop loss that will lock in profit as a trade develops. The stop loss indicates a price point at which the trader is prepared to admit that the trade is no longer valid and they're happy to close the position. A trading system can have multiple stop losses, as my breakout trading system does, but the bottom line is that the trader must always execute their stop loss strategy without failure. This is critical because risk management depends on it.

Now we'll delve a bit deeper by dissecting my active investing strategy into its component parts, but please be aware that this is by no means a full and comprehensive description of this trading system. For the full story on active investing, I recommend that you read my book *Active Investing* or visit my website <www.alanhull. com>, where you'll find a detailed set of explanatory notes. These notes can be downloaded for free and are in PDF format.

Trading premise

The trading premise for active investing is fairly straightforward. We assume that fundamentally sound blue chip shares that are rising in price will most likely continue to keep rising. Here's the explanation from the active investing notes on my website (throughout this chapter, I use excerpts from these notes, which appear in italics).

The simple dynamic that drives share prices either up or down is shown in figure 5.1.

Figure 5.1: the simple dynamic that drives share prices up or down

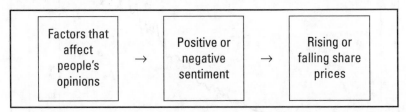

This diagram summarises the whole process that moves share prices and it is the basis of the active investing strategy. Factors that affect opinion include fundamentals, macroeconomics, global factors and more. So investors who

rely on fundamentals are coming at the market dynamic from the left-hand side. Chartists, on the other hand, are coming from the opposite direction by simply measuring the output of this whole dynamic process.

As active investors we will approach the market dynamic from both ends in order to identify blue chip shares in sustainable trends. Hence, there are blue chip shares that have good fundamentals and rising share prices and so we will search for shares that have both these attributes. Figure 5.2 shows the sorts of shares that we're looking for.

Figure 5.2: charts of Flight Centre (top) and Cochlear (bottom)

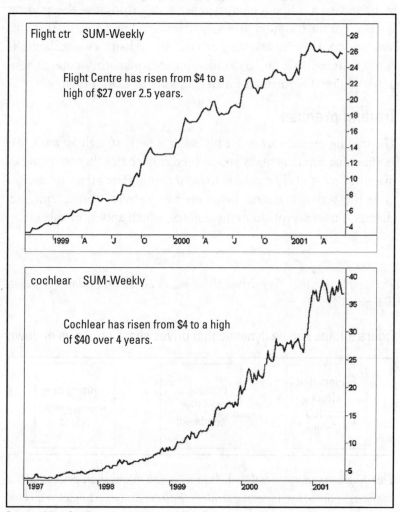

Source: MetaStock

Let's take a look at how fundamentalists view the market dynamic (see figure 5.3). Conventional investment wisdom ignores sentiment and assumes that if the financials and future prospects of a company are good then positive market sentiment can be assumed. This is absolutely true...given time. Hence the age-old reliance on having patience when it comes to investing.

Figure 5.3: if the financials and future prospects of a company are good, positive market setiment can be assumed

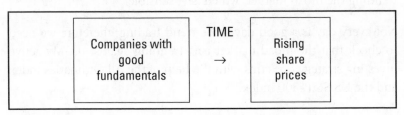

But by testing and measuring the market dynamic as active investors, we can largely eliminate the time factor and identify shares that are rising in price right now (see figure 5.4).

Figure 5.4: testing and measuring the market dynamic can identify shares that are rising in price

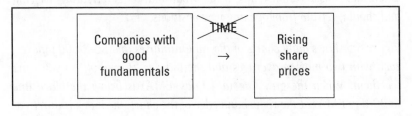

Note the robust and simplistic nature of this trading premise:

Good fundamentals + rising share price = sustainable trend

As we will be risking our money on the trading premise, we need to have absolute faith in it. This is very hard to do if it's not easily understood or it's a bit flaky. So the saying to remember here is 'keep it simple'.

Now that we've decided on our objective, we need to employ a set of filters that will help us find the shares we're looking for.

Search procedures

If we are trend trading (which we are in this instance) then there is a preliminary step we need to take and that is to check that the global market conditions are also moving in our favour. If you try to buy rising shares in a falling market then you are effectively counter-trending the broad market, which isn't sensible.

Not every day is a good day to be trend trading, therefore we need to check that the broad market isn't trending against us. My active investing strategy does this with the help of the All Ordinaries index and the US S&P-500 index.

Active investing assumes that sound fundamentals are the reason for share prices to be rising. But there are periods in the market cycle when other influences will control market sentiment and push factors such as good fundamentals, sound management and consistent profit growth into the background. Broad market sentiment is clearly one of them and must be taken into consideration. Thus, if the broad market is retreating, we can, and should, refrain from opening new positions.

Figure 5.5 shows daily charts of the All Ordinaries and S&P-500 indexes, each with two moving averages and the indexes 'turned off' so you can't see them. When the grey line (a 10-day EMA) is below the black line (a 30-day EMA) at the right-hand edge of the chart, the index is in retreat and trending down. And, inversely, when the grey line is above the black line then the index is trending upwards. These are commonly referred to as crossover charts.

A broad market decline is signalled when both of the indexes are retreating at the same time and when this happens you should refrain from opening any new positions. Any existing positions should be managed using their respective trailing stop losses. These 'crossover' charts act as a safety switch that prevents us from trading against the prevailing broad market trend and our own desire to have our money 100% committed to the market.

Figure 5.5: daily crossover charts of the All Ordinaries and S&P-500 indexes

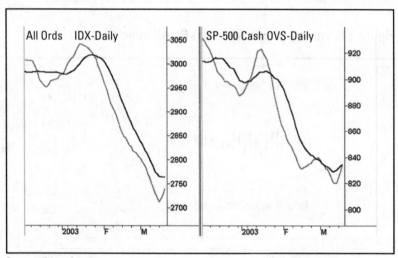

Source: MetaStock

If the broad market isn't in decline and it's okay to open new positions, we can start searching the market for fundamentally sound blue chip shares that are steadily rising in price. This requires the use of several different filters.

Locating blue chip shares with good fundamentals

Active investing employs a fundamental filter that uses a combination of criteria from two different sources. The fundamental search typically returns a list of about 150 shares.

- Top Stocks *by Martin Roth, published by Wrightbooks*
- StockDoctor *by Lincoln Indicators Pty Ltd (please visit <www.stockdoctor.com.au>)*

'Rate of annual return' searches

We then scan our group of fundamentally sound shares to locate the most profitable trading opportunities. We hold shares that are trending up with a rate of annual return (ROAR) of at least 20% but we only buy when the rate of annual return is at least 30%, as you can see in figure 5.6.

Figure 5.6: weekly price chart with ROAR indicator

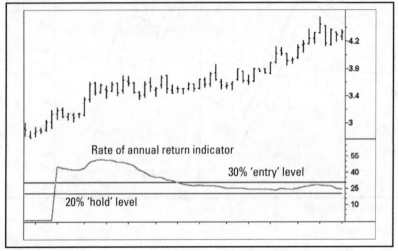

Rate of annual return indicator

30% 'entry' level

20% 'hold' level

Source: MetaStock

This 30% entry criteria combined with a 20% hold criteria provides a 10% buffer zone that prevents us from being whipsawed in and out of the market. For example, if we just used 30% as our entry and hold criteria and then if a share's rate of annual return fluctuated between 29% and 31%, we would be constantly buying and selling it — a scenario that we want to avoid.

Verifying and evaluating the trend

The final step is to ensure that a share is in a stable upward trend. In the early stages of a trend the long term set of lines on the MMA chart will initially compress and then expand as the trend gets under way. Once the trend is established, the long term MMA lines should be running parallel to each other and there should only be signs of relatively minor volatility (see figure 5.7).

Figure 5.7: MMA charts showing an acceptable trend (top) and unacceptable trend (bottom)

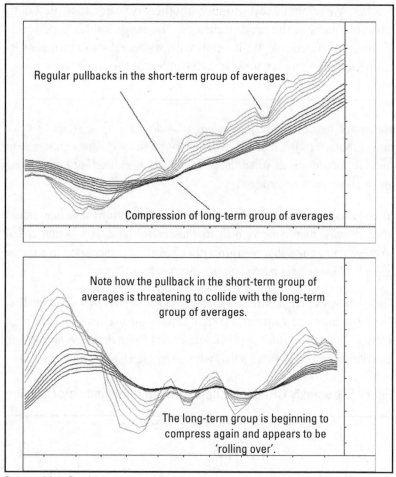

Source: MetaStock

As you can see, active investing employs three separate filters that search for fundamentally sound blue chip shares that are rising in price and have fairly low volatility. As you will discover in part II, my active trading strategy also employs a rate of return indicator and uses MMA charts for trend evaluation.

Entry trigger

The active investing strategy is in fact the active trading strategy's big brother. We're about to introduce another indicator that they both have in common: the range indicator. The range indicator performs a variety of functions. We'll begin with a general explanation of its construction before we look at the specifics of the entry trigger.

The range indicator (see figure 5.8) provides us with a series of price ranges that tell us when to buy, sell, hold or profit take. Although simple in construction, it tells us when the price activity is pulling back or rallying up, or the trend is reversing.

Its construction is based on an electronically generated line that tracks price activity, known henceforth as the central cord. A function called 'average true range' that measures price volatility is then used to position upper and lower lines based on the central cord.

These lines are referred to as the upper deviation line and lower deviation line. These two lines create an envelope that defines our tolerance towards price activity. The central cord, upper deviation and lower deviation lines create four distinct price zones that tell us when to buy, hold, take profit or sell.

Figure 5.8: weekly OHLC bar chart with the range indicator applied

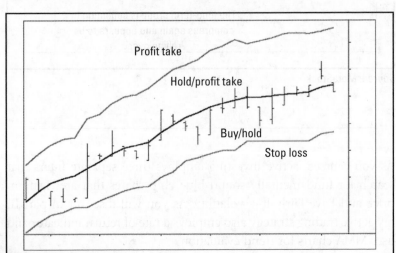

Source: MetaStock

By using the range indicator to control our entries and exits we can avoid buying overpriced shares and sell when a trend reversal occurs. If price rallies beyond the upper deviation line then there is a heightened probability that it will then fall past the lower deviation line. At this point investors and traders should sell and lock in profit.

That's a brief explanation of the range indicator's construction and its multipurpose use. Let's now drill down a bit deeper and look at how it's used for finetuning the market entry.

Once we have found a share that meets all our criteria and a ROAR greater than 30%, we must finetune the entry. Although we want to jump on board a trend when the price is in a dip, it is important not to enter the market while the price activity is falling or, putting it in colloquial terms, 'gunning the stop loss'. We need to wait for the market to reverse and turn upwards again, thus showing evidence of buyer support.

The green light is flashing after we have witnessed a rising week with a closing price higher than the previous week's close. When the green light is flashing we act on a daily basis and ensure that our buy price is in the buy zone; that is, equal to or below the central cord. Of course, it is possible for the 'market' to get away and so occasionally you will miss an opportunity to enter the market. Figure 5.9 (overleaf) shows a point of entry into a typical upward trend.

Thus, both the following criteria must be met in order for an entry to be signalled:

- *buyer support as evidenced by a closing price higher than the previous week's closing price*
- *price activity is in the 'Buy' zone.*

We will not be able to purchase an entire portfolio of shares immediately because many of the shares we want to buy won't be in the 'buy zone'. It is quite normal to spend quite a few weeks gradually buying into the market, catching each share as it dips down.

Figure 5.9: chart with range indicator showing an entry opportunity

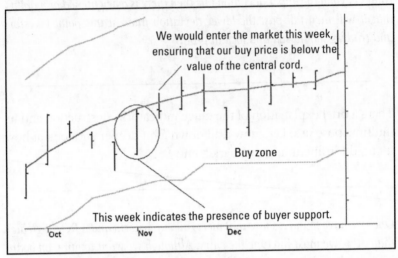

We would enter the market this week, ensuring that our buy price is below the value of the central cord.

Buy zone

This week indicates the presence of buyer support.

Oct   Nov   Dec

Source: MetaStock

After we've sifted through the market to find a small number of potential trading opportunities, we then have to patiently wait for an entry trigger from each share. Once we've bought into the market, we switch out of hunting mode and into management mode.

If you think the hardest part is behind you, think again. Many experienced traders will attest that trade management is far more critical to success than trade selection. Let's now move on to our reason for getting out of a trade—our exit criteria.

Exit criteria

Once again we need to return to the range indicator but this time it's not the buy zone that we're interested in.

When to exit the market is the most critical aspect of any strategy and the decision to sell must be simple, preferably mechanical and carried out with total discipline. Thus, when using the range indicator, if the price closes at the end of the week below the lower deviation, in the 'sell' zone, then you must immediately close out the position during the following week (see figure 5.10).

Figure 5.10: chart with range indicator showing an exit signal

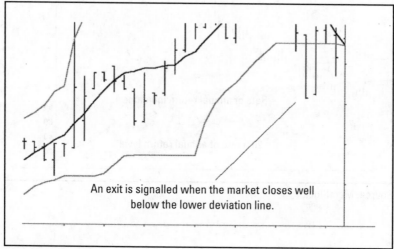

An exit is signalled when the market closes well
below the lower deviation line.

Source: MetaStock

Of course, if the price activity manages to rise up into the 'profit take' zone then a trader may elect to sell and take profit. However, profit taking is optional and may be completely overlooked or tempered by only selling half of a position rather than the entire holding.

But, along with the range indicator's 'sell' zone, the ROAR indicator also signals a mandatory exit if it drops below 20%. It is telling you that you are no longer trading a valid trend because the market has been moving sideways for too long. This type of exit criteria is what traders commonly refer to as a 'time based' stop loss. You can see in the following chart how the rate of annual return drops away when the market trades sideways for a prolonged period, signalling an exit condition when it falls below 20% (see figure 5.11, overleaf).

Thus, if either of the following criteria is met then a mandatory exit is signalled:

- *price activity has closed at the end of the week below the lower deviation*

- *the rate of annual return indicator has fallen below 20%.*

Figure 5.11: chart with ROAR indicator showing an exit signal

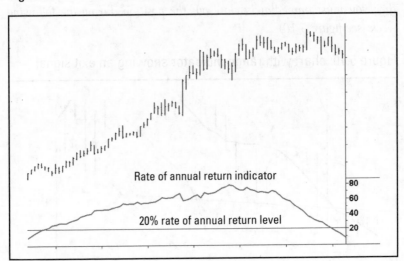

Source: MetaStock

So there you have it, a working trading system broken down into its key components:

- trading premise
- search procedures
- entry triggers
- exit criteria.

These four critical components, coupled with sound risk management, make up a complete trading system. Now you know what to look for when you go shopping for a readymade trading strategy or what critical aspects you need to consider if you want to design your own.

It all starts with the trading premise. If the trading premise is sound then you will most likely make money. But if it is invalid you will inevitably lose money. How you execute your trading premise is therefore less critical than the trading premise itself. Here's a simple saying to help you remember this:

Crawling in the right direction beats running in the wrong direction every time.

Share prices tend to trend and share prices cannot remain at rest indefinitely. These are my two key trading premises. In parts II and III, I show you exactly how I execute them so you know how to run in the right direction.

PART II

Active trading

Chapter 6

Introduction to active trading

We are now going to look at another fully road-tested trading system, but this time in much more detail. The system in question is the one I call active trading. Active trading is a short term, medium risk, *trend trading* system. Before I go into too much detail about the system, let me explain a bit more about price trends.

The trend is your friend

A well-known saying among traders, including yours truly, is 'the trend is your friend'. So who is this friend and what does it all mean? In the preface I covered what traders commonly accept as a universal fact —'markets tend to trend'—and in chapter 2 I looked at how to draw trend lines. I didn't actually define what a trend is, however, so let's take a step back for a moment and describe what constitutes a trend (these definitions are from my book *Charting in a Nutshell*):

- an upward trend occurs when price activity moves upward from the left of a chart to the right

- a downward trend is where price activity moves downward from left to right.

For active trading I am after only relatively short-term trends and therefore I only want to analyse several months' worth of price activity. Let's take a look at a couple of examples, starting with a candlestick chart with an upward trend (see figure 6.1), then one with a downward trend (see figure 6.2). In both figures I've included fairly casually placed trend lines just to reinforce the direction of the prevailing trend.

Figure 6.1: candlestick chart of share with trend line indicating an upward trend

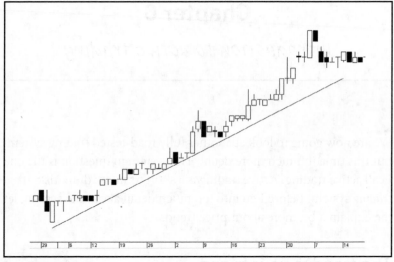

Source: MetaStock

Since we accept that 'markets tend to trend', it is vital for us to be able to identify a trend in a time frame that is relevant to our style of trading or investing, particularly if we want our system to be profitable! Providing we do this, trend trading is the most universally acknowledged successful premise for trading financial markets, especially shares. It therefore makes sense to me to use trend trading as the basis of one of my short-term share trading systems.

Another key feature of trend trading that makes it so attractive is that it is a relatively simple style of trading to implement. I therefore employ it on a short-term basis in my active trading strategy or system and also in the longer term in my active investing system, which I briefly described in chapter 5.

Figure 6.2: candlestick chart of share with trend line indicating a downward trend

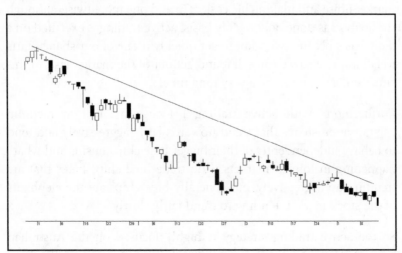

Source: MetaStock

What is active trading?

Active trading was released in 2004 and is a shorter-term version of active investing. It is a short-term, trend-based system for trading equity markets. While it could be retuned to trade other financial markets, the bulk of my experience is with equity markets and I firmly believe in sticking to what you're familiar with. Active trading can be used to trade both sides of the market (that is, rising and falling shares), but I employ it to trade only rising shares. There are limited derivatives available for short selling most of the equities traded on the Australian stock market, so while the strategy is quite capable of producing short selling opportunities, you would find yourself frustrated by a lack of suitable trading instruments. Furthermore, you will find that trend trading falling markets is generally less successful than trend trading rising markets.

To trade shares solely on their technical merits, or come as close as possible, it is necessary to work in a reasonably short time frame, so active trading is a short-term approach. By operating in this time frame, we largely avoid the impact of other factors such as company fundamentals and macroeconomic influences because their impact is generally felt over the longer term.

On the other hand, this short-term trading system is based on weekly analysis rather than daily analysis, helping to filter out random market noise and making life easier. To add one more twist, although the analysis is done on a weekly basis, active trading is executed on a daily basis because we want to act quickly if one of our shares starts to fall in price so we can sell it and get out of the market fast. In this situation, a week can be a very long time!

Furthermore, with active trading I focus on small to medium capitalisation shares that trend upwards fairly aggressively and tend to behave independently of their bigger blue chip cousins and what's happening in foreign markets. I do trade blue chip shares that are trending up aggressively, but generally blue chips are the elephants of the stock market, tending to trend fairly slowly.

So the active trading strategy is highly focused on the Australian stock market and the factors that influence it, such as the local economy and demand for our exports. Although it is targeted at small to medium-capitalisation shares, it is also prudent to take into consideration the state of the entire market as well. To do this, we analyse the All Ordinaries index and the Small Ordinaries index.

Markets don't always trend up and down

Before we drill down into the specifics of the active trading strategy, here's an important caveat about trend trading in general. So far I've shown you some pristine examples of trending markets, but in reality markets don't always trend. It therefore logically follows that we can't always be in the market as trend traders because there are simply times when there are no opportunities, particularly if we are trading in only one direction—up. Every day is not a good day to trend trade as markets are NOT always trending up!

Figure 6.3 is long-term chart showing one and a half years of the All Ordinaries index. We can see that overall the trend is upward.

However, if we took a small section from this chart to analyse, then our view changes. In figure 6.4 we're looking at six months of the All Ordinaries index. Here, the market looks like it's trending sideways to downwards. The active trading strategy works in this shorter time frame, so it would probably perform fairly poorly during this period.

Figure 6.3: the All Ordinaries index from late 2005 to early 2007

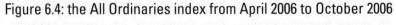

Source: MetaStock

Figure 6.4: the All Ordinaries index from April 2006 to October 2006

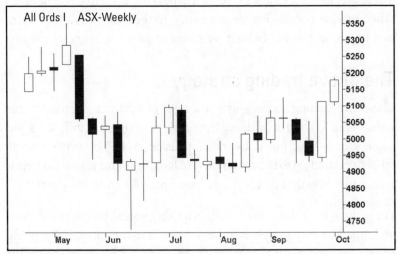

Source: MetaStock

When we examine markets in any particular time frame, we find that they have three gears: up, down and sideways. Obviously, the first thing we need to do is make sure we are looking at an appropriate period of time in our charts for our particular system. We then need to make sure when we are trend trading that the market is actually trending in the direction that we are trading in.

It's an unfortunate fact that there will be times when the market is in the wrong gear and it is very important that not only can we recognise this, but we know what to do when it happens. A fatal mistake is to trade against the trend. This is when the market is trending in the opposite direction to what our system requires, but we go ahead and trade anyway. While we'll live to tell the tale, our back pocket nerves will receive a severe hammering!

Another, slightly lesser, mistake is to trend trade even though the market is NOT trending. Again, we'll certainly live to tell the tale, but our bank balance will either not move or be slowly eroded. Your stockbroker will be happy as they still receive their commissions whether you make money or not. Thus, active trading is not a universal trading solution and should be employed only when market conditions support it.

The critical point here is that markets will NOT always be trending in the direction that we want them to! So when the market is not 'playing ball', trend traders have to learn to just sit on the sidelines. There are, however, other systems that can be used to trade in times when market conditions are not suited to the active trading system, and breakout trading (which we cover in part III) is one of them.

The active trading strategy

The active trading strategy uses a weight of evidence approach. This means I am looking at evidence from a range of different indicators and sources from which to draw my conclusion(s). In fact, active trading takes trend trading to the extreme as I'm looking for trends within trends within trends within trends. That's four layers of trends, to be precise!

I'm looking for a rising market, then a rising sector, then a rising share and, finally, a rising week. For the remainder of this chapter, I'm going to explain each of these four layers. In chapter 7 I'll detail the tools I use to measure each one of them. The logical place to start is with the top layer; the state of the entire Australian stock market.

Rising market indexes

Rising market indexes is my first layer of evidence. In the active trading strategy, I analyse the broader market using both the All Ords and the Small Ords indexes. My first layer of evidence is to make sure that the broad market represented by the All Ords index is rising (see figure 6.5). Then I also need to make sure that the particular index that represents the small to medium capitalisation shares, such as the Small Ords, is also rising (see figure 6.6).

Figure 6.5: weekly candlestick chart of the All Ordinaries index

Source: MetaStock

Figure 6.6: weekly candlestick chart of the Small Ordinaries index

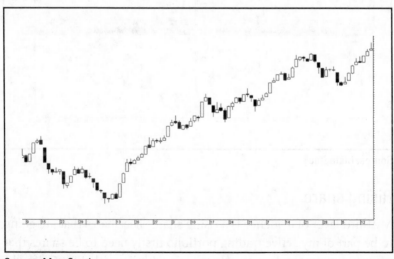

Source: MetaStock

Rising sector

The next layer is the rising sector. What I am looking for here is a sector or sectors that are rising the fastest. I want to hunt for shares in the fastest rising sectors, providing they have an acceptably low level of volatility. Of course, I'll employ sector risk to balance out my portfolio and make sure that I limit my total exposure to each particular sector.

This means that I will need to look at trading shares from about three or four different sectors to spread the risk far enough. However, this shouldn't prove too much of a problem because there are 22 global industry classification standard (GICS) industry group sectors to choose from. These 22 different sectors form the backdrop for my rising sector analysis and the charts in figure 6.7 show some examples of these sectors.

Figure 6.7: line-on-close charts of some GICS industry group sectors

Source: MetaStock

Rising share

My third layer of evidence is a rising share. The shares that are going to be part of my active trading portfolio firstly need to be shares that are trending upwards in the short term with low volatility. Secondly, they will also need to be rising at an acceptable rate and we'll look into this in more detail in chapter 7.

We want steadily upward trending shares as well as shares that will go up nice and quickly! Figure 6.8 is an example of a relatively smooth, yet rapidly upward trending share that we would consider acceptable.

Figure 6.8: candlestick chart of a rising share

Source: MetaStock

Rising week, or upweek

A rising week is my last layer of evidence. After getting through the previous three layers and having identified a particular share or shares, I will now enter the market only when a share has been rising for at least the last week. I'm doing this because I don't want to buy a share when it is falling in the very short term. I want a share that is showing immediate strength, so I want to witness what we call 'buyer support'. One obvious way in which buyer support is evident is when a share closes at the end of the week higher than it closed at the end of the previous week; that is, an 'upweek' (see figure 6.9, overleaf).

In summary, with my active trading system I'm seeking:

1   a rising market as indicated by both the All Ordinaries (All Ords) and Small Ordinaries (Small Ords)

2   a rising sector or sectors that are trending up with relatively low volatility

3   a rising share that is trending up very rapidly but with relatively low volatility

4   an upweek where the closing price is higher than the previous week's closing price.

Figure 6.9: candlestick chart showing an upweek where the close is higher than the previous week's close

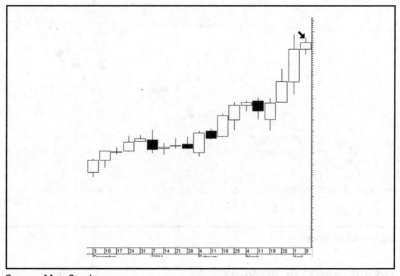

Source: MetaStock

These are the four layers that form the basis of my active trading system. It is a top-down approach to trading where we start off with the big picture, then work our way down. In chapter 7, I explain the tools I use to assess each of these layers.

Chapter 7

Tools of the trade for active trading

Now we're going to get down to the nitty gritty of the active trading system. In chapter 6, I explained the basic design of this strategy. In this chapter, I explain how I measure each of the four trends that make up the system. We examine all of the tools I employ in detail, which are:

- rising indexes—we use moving average crossover charts, namely 10- and 30-day exponential moving averages (EMAs)

- rising sector—we use sector multiple moving averages (MMA) charts and my rate of return (RoR) indicator

- rising share—we use share MMA charts and my RoR indicator

- upweek—we analyse weekly price data to determine this condition.

I also use my range indicator, which we discussed in chapter 5, when we examined trade management.

We'll start at the upper or outermost layer, the analysis of the All Ords and Small Ords indexes.

Rising index

I use the simple yet very effective crossover chart to determine the direction of the trend of both the All Ords and the Small Ords. Figure 7.1 shows the crossover charts for the two indexes. Note that I have turned the index off in each case so you can see only the two moving averages.

Figure 7.1: All Ords (top) and Small Ords (below) crossover charts

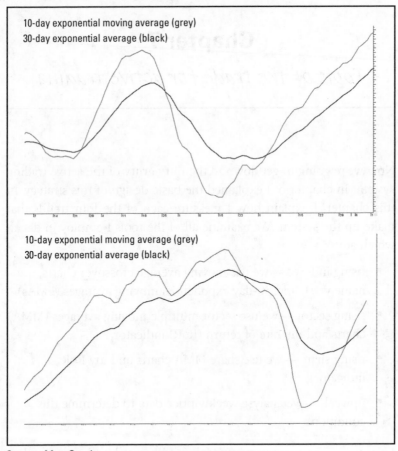

10-day exponential moving average (grey)
30-day exponential average (black)

10-day exponential moving average (grey)
30-day exponential average (black)

Source: MetaStock

Here I'm looking at two short-term moving averages applied to daily charts of the All Ords and the Small Ords. The lighter of the two lines (the fast moving average of the two) is a 10-day exponential moving average (EMA) and the black line (the slower moving average) is a

30-day EMA. I chose these moving averages and particular periods because I have determined through many years of trialling different combinations that this is the most suitable combination for assessing the direction of the Australian stock market for my given time frame.

The rules for interpreting the crossover charts are *very* simple. *Both* of the charts must be crossed to the upside; that is, the grey line must be above the black line at the right-hand leading edge of the chart, in both cases. A chart is therefore crossed in a particular direction when the grey line (the shorter of the two moving averages) is *above* or *below* the black line at the right-hand leading edge of the chart. If the grey line is above the black line, then the chart is crossed to the upside. If the grey line is below the black line, the chart is crossed to the downside. If the two lines are sitting on top of each other at the right-hand leading edge then they are not crossed in either direction.

These charts are my starting point, so we need to be very clear on their interpretation. If I can look at both charts and see a grey line above the black line and I am looking to buy shares, I know that the indicator is telling me that I have the green light for go or, as attendees of one of my trading workshops will have heard me say, 'let's go shopping'!

This is the first stage of the system and is a vital step because if we attempt to countertrend the broad market by trading against it, we will surely fail. The crossover charts provide us with clear, unambiguous signals. However, in the next stage we will see some discretion start to come into the trading process.

Rising sector

I use two tools to help pick which sectors I'm going to look at. The first tool is an MMA chart that lets me pick sectors with suitable trends. The second tool is a rate of return indicator, or RoR. This shows me which of the sectors are rising or falling at the fastest rates.

Sector MMAs

I'm using the GICS industry group sectors as the basis of my sector analysis. My indicator of choice here is the MMAs (as discussed in chapter 3) for assessing the quality of trends. Figure 7.2 shows what they look like.

Figure 7.2: GICS industry group sectors with MMAs

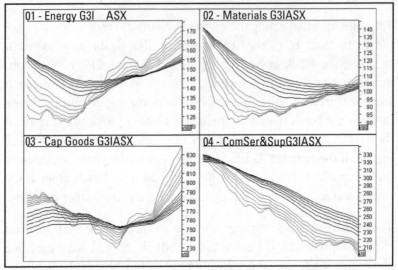

Source: MetaStock

Here we can see four of the 22 main sectors over about a 30-week period. The shorter term group of averages (the grey lines) is 3, 5, 7, 9, 11 and 13 periods and the longer term group (black lines) is 21, 24, 27, 30, 33 and 36 periods. All moving averages are exponential and the periodicity used is weekly. Again, I've hidden the price activity for ease of reading.

This is a discretionary part of the analysis, but the MMAs show me which sectors have the valid trends I'm looking for as part of this stage of the process. These charts do a great job at filtering out the short-term noise of the market so I can focus on what the actual underlying trend is doing.

I'm looking for nice trends; those that have been rising for at least two months and have an acceptable low level of volatility. Note that we use the same type of analysis here that we are going to use when we look at the MMA charts of individual shares. It is therefore very important that we are as discerning with our analysis of the MMA charts for the sectors as we are with the shares.

Following is a list of critical points to consider when interpreting the MMA charts:

- The long-term group must be pointing upwards.

- The long-term group must be spreading apart or running parallel with each other.

- The straighter the long-term group of lines is, the less volatile the trend is.

- The short-term group can pull back (compress) but shouldn't come into contact with the long-term group of averages and preferably the pull backs should be regular.

Now I have narrowed it down to the sectors with valid trends, I have to narrow it further to those rising the fastest. To do this I'm going to introduce a new indicator, the rate of return indicator.

Rate of return indicator (RoR)

The rate of return (ROR) indicator is used to calculate the annual rate of return of a share or an index (such as a sector index), given its current rate of climb or fall. In simple terms, we take the annual change of the share or sector, divide it by the current value of the share or sector and multiply by 100 to convert the figure to a percentage. For example, say a sector is rising at a rate of 120 points per year; that is, the change in value over 12 months is 120 points. The current value of the sector index is 1980 points. The annual RoR would therefore be 0.061 (120/1980). To convert this to a percentage we multiply by 100 and get 6 per cent (rounded off).

If we apply this measurement to all the sectors with valid trends, we can see which ones are moving the fastest, and these are the ones we want. Now let's get a little more specific about the design of the RoR indicator. Rather than use the change in value over one year, which is a little blunt, we take a three-month sample and then annualise the result. To provide a degree of smoothing, our values are taken from a 26-week Hull moving average (HMA), rather than the actual price activity itself. The charts in figure 7.3 (overleaf) show the sector MMAs and also the RoR values at the top of each chart window. Note that if the RoR is negative it means that the sector is falling.

Figure 7.3: GICS industry group sectors with MMAs and RoR

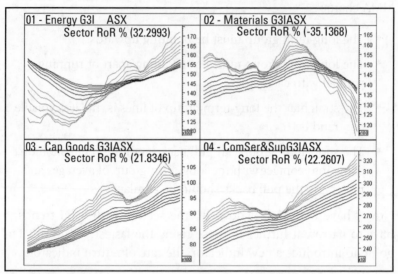

Source: MetaStock

At this point I usually pick out the top three or four sectors, providing that there are that many acceptable ones. I have to consider my sector risk management rules and therefore I need to spread my portfolio over at least three sectors. If I can't find enough acceptable sectors, I might be forced to leave some of my money in the bank ... alas, risk management is non-negotiable.

Now I have the tools to not only find the sectors with valid trends, but I can also find the ones that are rising the fastest. So what's next? Now we get down to the sharp end of the process because it's time to look for those rising shares in the rising sectors.

Rising shares

The process for identifying rising shares is very similar to that used to identify rising sectors. Again the two tools to be used will be MMA charts and the RoR indicator. At this point I'm trying to find the most suitable shares in the sectors I identified in the previous step. The MMA charts will show me the shares with the valid trends and the RoR will let me know which ones are rising the fastest. First, let's take a look at some share MMA charts (see figure 7.4).

Figure 7.4: share charts with MMAs

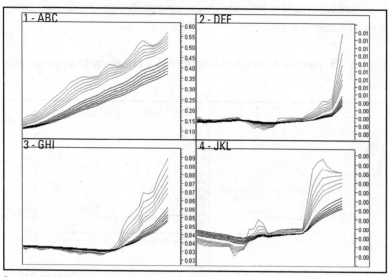

Source: MetaStock

Again I'm using weekly charts with the following EMAs:

- short-term group (grey lines) is 3, 5, 7, 9, 11 and 13
- long-term group (black lines) is 21, 24, 27, 30, 33 and 36.

We use the same rules for interpreting the share MMA charts that we used for the sector MMA charts, making sure we remember the critical points listed previously. Figure 7.5 (overleaf) shows a few examples of the good, the bad and the ugly!

As we did with the sectors, we apply the RoR indicator to the shares to make sure the trends are rising fast enough. Because this is a short-term system, we want fast moving shares with high RoR. For this system, I'm going to set my RoR minimum to 80 per cent. This means that if the weekly value of a share's RoR is below 80 per cent, I'll sell that share and replace it with another, if there's a suitable opportunity. This ensures that my money is always working hard for me and I'm not holding onto shares that are just drifting sideways.

One more thing I need is a minimum entry RoR to ensure that I'm not whipsawed in and out of the market if a share's RoR hovers just above and below 80 per cent. Having a minimum entry RoR of 120 per cent provides a buffer zone of 40 per cent (120 per cent − 80 per cent). Figure 7.6 is a chart of a share with the RoR indicator (in the uppermost window) so you can see how it changes over time.

Figure 7.5: sample of various share MMA charts with appropriate titles!

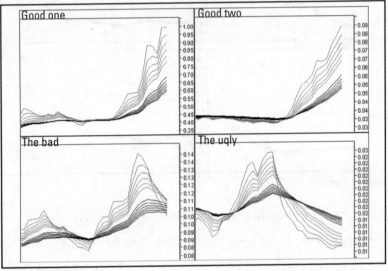

Source: MetaStock

Figure 7.6: candlestick chart of share and RoR indicator (RoR scaled by 10)

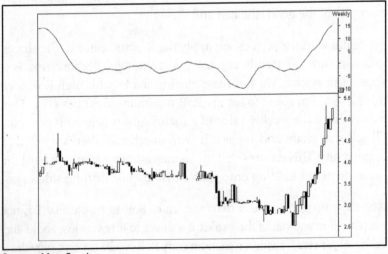

Source: MetaStock

Applying the RoR to the shares with valid trends gives me a list of the best possible candidates for my portfolio. Once we've narrowed the search to this degree, we're ready to complete the last step in the process and find the shares with rising weeks or upweeks. Once we've done so, we can finetune our entry and call the broker!

Rising week or upweek

In chapter 5 we discussed the range indicator because it is used in my active investing strategy as well (note that it is tuned slightly differently because it's being applied to only blue chip shares in that instance). The range indicator, as well as plain old end-of-week closing prices, enables us to find the shares with a valid entry.

Finding if a share has had an upweek is really very simple. All we need to do is look at the current end-of-week closing price (remember, our analysis is weekly), then look at the closing price from last week. If this week's closing price is greater than last week's closing price, this week is an upweek. Note that if the prices are the same, it is not an upweek! Table 7.1 lists a few examples—see if you can pick out the shares with an upweek.

Table 7.1: table of shares showing closing price for this week and last week

Share code	Closing price this week ($)	Closing price last week ($)
MNO	3.220	3.000
PQR	0.230	0.310
STU	0.355	0.354
VWX	0.625	0.625
YZA	1.135	1.250

Yes, there were only two (MNO and STU); the others are either down or neutral. Once we've sorted out which ones had an upweek, we can use the range indicator to find out if we have a valid entry.

Range indicator

The range indicator provides us with a series of price ranges that tell us when to buy, sell, hold or take profit. Although simple in construction, it tells us when the price activity is pulling back or rallying up, or the trend is reversing. Like the RoR indicator, its construction is based on the Hull moving average, referred to in this context as the central cord.

We use average true range (which, if you recall, measures price volatility) to position upper and lower lines based on the central cord. These lines are referred to as the upper deviation line and lower deviation line. These two lines create an envelope that defines our tolerance towards price volatility.

The central cord, upper deviation and lower deviation lines create four distinct price zones that tell us when to buy, hold, profit take or sell. The chart in figure 7.7 illustrates how the range indicator is used to set buy, hold and sell zones.

Figure 7.7: share chart showing range indicator

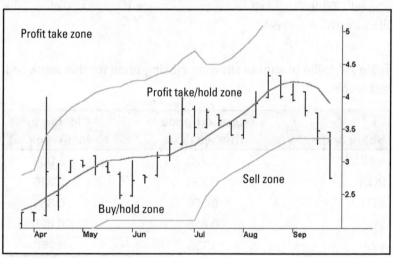

Source: MetaStock

The rules for the zones are:

- sell zone—sell if the share closes the day in this zone.
- buy/hold zone—buy the share if it has closed at the end of the week in this zone and the price is higher than the previous

week's closing price. The share must be purchased at a price between the lower deviation and the central cord. Hold if already owned.

- profit take/hold zone—hold if the share price is in this zone or take profits if the position is up strongly from its initial purchase price (maybe sell half of the position).

- profit take zone—mandatory: take profits if the share price closes at the end of the week in this zone (in this instance sell the entire position). Optional: take profits if the share price is in this zone at any time.

When price activity trends it moves in a sawtooth pattern, not a straight line. In an upward trend this behaviour is caused by the repetition of a rally/pull back cycle. As long as the buying force behind the rallies is greater than the selling force behind the pull backs, the trend will continue. Upward trends end when the buying force is exhausted, which is an inevitable occurrence. Share traders often forget that all trends must ultimately end.

By using the range indicator to control our entries and exits we can avoid buying overpriced shares and sell when a trend reversal occurs. Although the range indicator is applied to weekly charts (that is, weekly analysis), the buy and sell signals are applied on a day-to-day basis (that is, daily execution).

Table 7.2 (overleaf) lists shares where you can see whether or not they have had an upweek by looking at the third column. It also shows the range and RoR indicator values, so we can work out which ones have a valid entry and which ones don't. Note that the RoR indicator measures a share's rate of annual return which I refer to in the table as the ROAR value.

Share FFF is a valid entry as long as we purchase it at a price between the lower deviation and the central cord. Unfortunately, the share price may suddenly take off and we may not be able to purchase it in the buy zone, so we'd have to wait for another opportunity. It is quite normal to spend several weeks or more waiting for entry signals to completely fill an active trading portfolio.

Table 7.2: list of shares showing weekly direction, range indicator and RoR indicator values

Share code	Closing price ($)	Up/down week	Central cord ($)	Upper deviation ($)	Lower deviation ($)	ROAR (%)
AAA	0.255	Up	0.258	0.266	0.244	184
BBB	0.670	Down	0.791	0.923	0.579	157
CCC	3.610	Up	3.688	3.922	3.309	110
DDD	0.096	Up	0.102	0.120	0.074	137
EEE	0.620	Up	0.748	0.860	0.568	116
FFF	0.435	Up	0.516	0.607	0.370	174
GGG	0.715	Down	0.821	1.009	0.517	248
HHH	3.220	Up	3.350	3.508	3.094	81
III	0.230	Down	0.256	0.305	0.175	137
JJJ	0.355		0.462	0.555	0.311	204
KKK	0.625	Up	0.822	0.978	0.569	231

Trade management

When you've found a share you want to buy you need to work out your position size. To do this you need to know your buy price and your initial stop loss to apply the 2 per cent risk rule (we discussed this in chapter 4). Of course, the lower deviation will be your stop loss. Remember that your maximum position size must never exceed 20 per cent of your total capital, no matter what.

We already know that if a share's RoR drops below 80 per cent, it has to be sold, but there are other times when we will have to sell a share. As you saw a little earlier, the range indicator has a sell zone. If a share has an end-of-day close below the lower deviation, we must sell that share. There is no negotiating with this rule!

So that's the active trading system; the hows and whys behind it, and the tools needed to implement the system. You will find the MetaStock formulas for all of the indicators described in this chapter in appendix A. There's a lot to digest in this chapter so it may take multiple readings to fully grasp all the workings of the strategy.

Now, to take the strategy for a test drive, I'm going to hand over to Simon Sherwood for chapter 8, where he's going to run through a simulation using my active trading newsletter. This newsletter is the commercial version of the system I've outlined in the last two chapters. You'll see how it all pieces together as he applies the strategy over several weeks of market activity.

Chapter 8

Taking active trading for a test drive

This chapter was written by Simon Sherwood, who assists with the weekly production of both my active investing and active trading newsletters.

We've read about the theory of active trading. Now it's time to see it work in real time. To simulate how the strategy works, we're going to use the *Active Trading Newsletter* for all the charts and data and the ActVest Trade Recorder to track our portfolio. The ActVest Trade Recorder is a simple Excel-based spreadsheet tool that contains all the information we need to track our portfolio without distracting us with too much clutter!

We follow these steps:

1 check the stop losses for all our open positions (very important, this should be the FIRST thing we do each week)

2 check the crossover charts

3 select suitable sector MMA charts with the highest rates of return

4 select suitable share MMA charts

5 check share data tables for valid entries

6 calculate purchase details and position size

7 update records.

We do this over four weeks, starting on 2 February 2007.

Week 1

This is the beginning of the simulation, so the first thing we need to do is to set up our ActVest Trade Recorder. We're going to start with $100 000 cash. The first newsletter we're looking at is AT070202 (where the numbers reference the date—YYMMDD), so we'll set up our Trade Recorder so it looks like figure 8.1.

Figure 8.1: ActVest Trade Recorder showing cash and newsletter reference

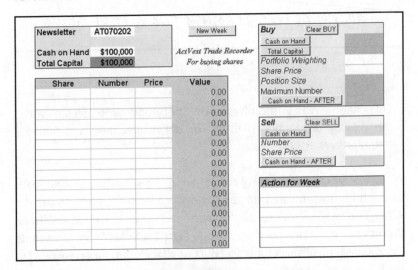

When we get to the stage of clicking the 'New Week' button, the macros in the spreadsheet will save the file under the name of the newsletter reference; that is, AT070202.xls. This way we can easily match the appropriate spreadsheet with the corresponding newsletter. The other benefit of the ActVest Trade Recorder is that it contains only the information we need—cash on hand, the share codes and the number of shares. Of course, as we progress through this simulation you'll get a much better idea of how the spreadsheet works.

Usually the first step would be to check our stop losses, but because this is week 1, we don't have any open positions so there's nothing to check.

Our second step is to check the crossover charts. We're looking at the All Ords and the Small Ords to get the green light to go shopping. We need *both* of them crossed to the upside (as explained in chapter 7). The two charts from our first newsletter are shown in figure 8.2.

Figure 8.2: All Ords crossover chart (top) and Small Ords crossover chart (below)

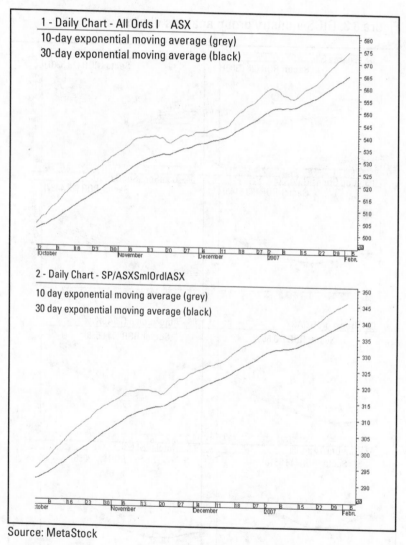

Source: MetaStock

Both of these charts are crossed to the upside because the grey line is above the black line for both charts. So, as Alan says, let's go shopping!

Well, almost—now we have to look at our next level, which is the sector MMA charts.

Here we are looking for suitable rising sectors and this is what they look like (all 22 of the GICS industry group MMA charts are shown in figure 8.3). Remember that suitable MMA charts are those that have been rising for at least two months and have an acceptable low level of volatility.

Figure 8.3: GICS industry group analysis charts

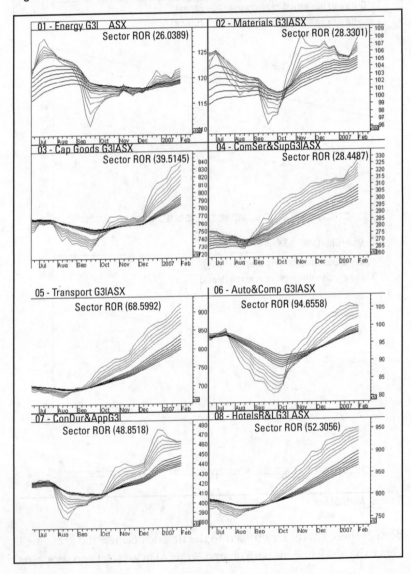

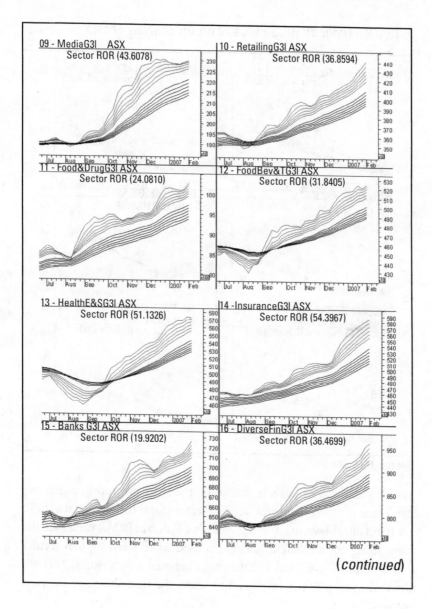

(*continued*)

Figure 8.3 (*cont'd*): GICS industry group analysis charts

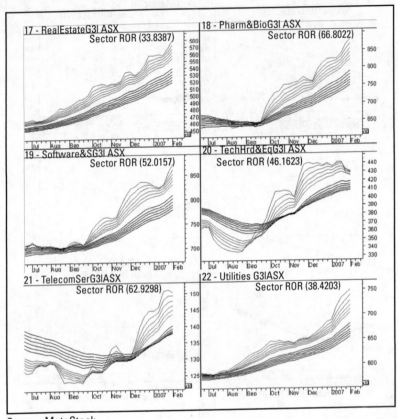

Source: MetaStock

Looking at the MMA charts and using the rules previously stated, we can come up with the list of suitable sectors (and their respective RoR, rounded off) shown in table 8.1. Note that RoR and ROAR values are the same thing but a different notation is used when referring to a sector's rate of return (ROR) and a share's rate of annual return (ROAR). That's the end of step 3; now we need to select the best shares in the best sectors.

For this particular week, there are more than 170 charts of shares with a ROAR more than 80 per cent, so we'll look at a sample of them (see figure 8.4), then move on to the shares I've selected for the simulation. If you want to see a recent sample of an active trading (ActTrade) newsletter with all its charts and data, send a request to us at enquiries@alanhull.com.

Table 8.1: suitable sectors and their respective RoR

GICS industry group	ROR %
Transport	69
Pharm & biotech	67
Insurance	54
Software & services	52
Utilities	38
Retailing	37
Diverse	36
Real estate	34
Food bev & tobacco	32

Figure 8.4: sample of weekly MMA charts from the ActTrade Newsletter

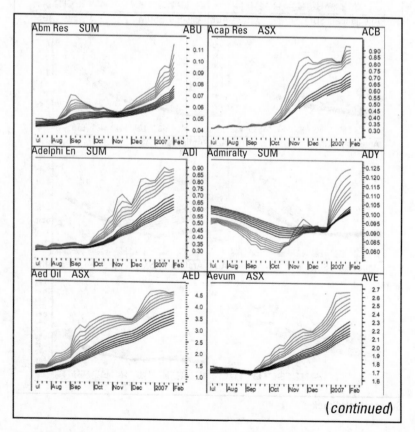

(*continued*)

Figure 8.4 (*cont'd*): sample of weekly MMA charts from the ActTrade Newsletter

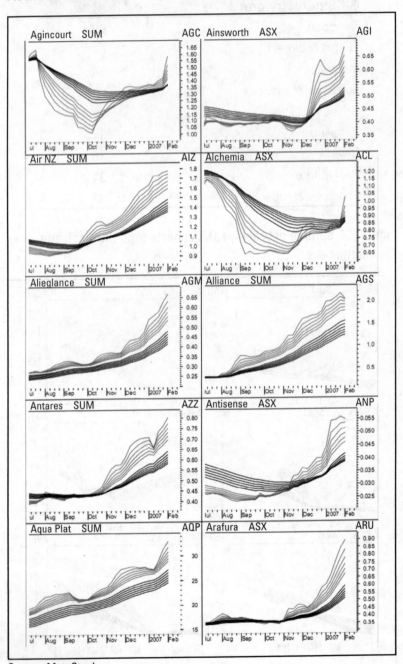

Source: MetaStock

From examining all of the 177 MMA charts, we've come up with the short list of suitable shares shown in table 8.2. We've narrowed our search to those sectors listed earlier, so now we have a short list of upward trending shares in the upward trending sectors.

Table 8.2: upward trending shares in the upward trending sectors

SHARE	GICS industry group
MRM	Transportation
REX	Transportation
TOL	Transportation
VBA	Transportation
CUV	Pharmaceuticals & biotechnology
PWT	Software & services
UXC	Software & services
HGI	Diversified financials
GPN	Real estate
SDG	Real estate
TGR	Food, beverage & tobacco

From this short list we can move to the next step, which is to check for valid entries. For this we refer to the weekly ActTrade data tables, a sample of which is shown in figure 8.5.

Figure 8.5: sample of ActTrade Newsletter data tables

ActTrade **Rising Equities**

Share Code	Closing Price ($)	Central Cord ($)	Upper ($) Deviation	Lower ($) Deviation	ROAR (%)	Port. Weighting for the 2% risk
AAX	4.880	4.878	5.550	3.790	108	9
ABU	0.135	0.138	0.165	0.094	149	6
ACB	0.920	1.017	1.064	0.940	158	20
ACL	1.195	1.191	1.327	0.971	97	11
ADI	0.900	1.013	1.118	0.842	166	18
ADY	0.125	0.140	0.158	0.111	106	11
AED	4.700	5.502	6.191	4.387	91	17
AEE	0.690	0.721	0.892	0.445	234	5
AGC	1.750	1.901	2.039	1.678	87	20
AGI	0.750	0.967	1.145	0.679	131	11
AGM	0.705	0.766	0.906	0.538	153	8
AGS	1.910	2.349	2.688	1.801	184	11
AIZ	1.790	1.960	2.206	1.562	112	13
AKK	0.820	1.025	1.206	0.733	217	9
ANG	1.370	1.538	1.750	1.195	168	11
ANP	0.054	0.066	0.078	0.047	168	9
AOE	1.220	1.249	1.338	1.106	116	18

The data tables also include two additional columns that show the GICS industry group and the weekly direction: 'up' if this week's closing price is higher than last week's closing price, 'dn' if it is lower, and a blank if there is no change (due to space restrictions I've left these two columns out).

Now we'll sort our prospects by their ROAR value to see which are the best candidates and ensure they pass all the entry criteria:

- an up week
- ROAR > = 120 per cent
- closing price in the buy zone, which means it must be less than or equal to the value of the central cord and greater than or equal to the value of the lower deviation.

Our list of prospects is shown in table 8.3.

Table 8.3: list of prospects showing entry criteria

Share	GICS industry group		ROAR %	Buy zone
REX	Transportation	Up	129	in
MRM	Transportation	Up	128	in
VBA	Transportation	—	98	
TOL	Transportation	Up	80	
CUV	Pharmaceuticals & biotechnology	Up	156	in
PWT	Software & services	Up	152	in
UXC	Software & services	Up	93	
HGI	Diversified financials	Up	98	
GPN	Real estate	Up	202	in
SDG	Real estate	Dn		
TGR	Food, beverage & tobacco	Up	86	

If we then eliminate the shares that don't meet our criteria — those where the ROAR is less than 120 per cent, or the weekly direction is *not* up, or the weekly closing price is *not* in the buy zone — we are left with our final list (see table 8.4).

Table 8.4: final list of prospects that meet all our criteria

Share	GICS industry group		ROAR %	Buy zone
REX	Transportation	Up	129	in
MRM	Transportation	Up	128	in
CUV	Pharmaceuticals & biotechnology	Up	156	in
PWT	Software & services	Up	152	in
GPN	Real estate	Up	202	in

The respective entries in the data tables are shown in table 8.5. Note the column on the far right of the data tables with the heading 'Port. weighting for the 2% risk', which stands for 'Portfolio weighting for the 2 per cent risk rule'. We've calculated the percentage of your total capital that you can allocate to each share in order to risk only 2 per cent of your total capital. This figure is based on the lower deviation and the closing price.

Table 8.5: respective entries in the data tables for prospects that meet all our criteria

Share code	Closing price ($)	Central cord ($)	Upper deviation ($)	Lower deviation ($)	ROAR (%)	Port. weighting for the 2% risk
CUV	0.895	1.012	1.195	0.716	156	8
GPN	0.053	0.053	0.066	0.033	202	5
MRM	1.200	1.270	1.451	0.978	128	10
PWT	2.270	2.438	2.778	1.888	152	10
REX	2.070	2.282	2.646	1.694	129	9

The MMA charts we earlier (see table 8.2 on p. 115) used to narrow down our prospects are shown in figure 8.6 (overleaf).

Figure 8.6: weekly MMA charts from the ActTrade newsletter

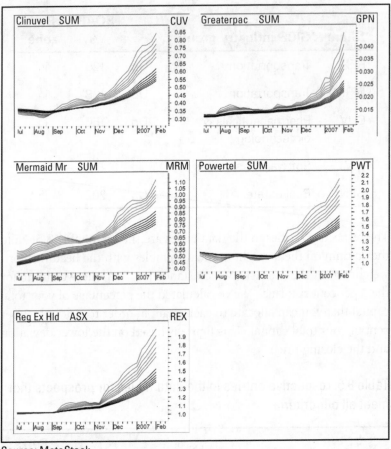

Source: MetaStock

We're now ready to work out our position sizes and enter our trades in the Trade Recorder. To keep this exercise reasonably simple, we're going to use the weekly closing price listed in the newsletter data tables as our actual buy price.

We'll start with the best performing share in the best performing sector and work our way down from there. Utilising the BUY calculator in the Trade Recorder and the figures from the data tables, you can see that we can purchase 4347 shares of REX (see figure 8.7). To understand what we've done here you can revisit our final list of prospects and the data tables to see where we got the information for the calculator.

Figure 8.7: Trade Recorder buy calculator for REX

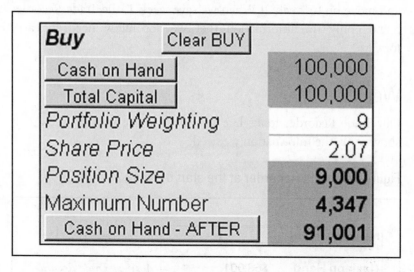

Now we'll go ahead and do the calculations for the rest of the shares, so we end up with the information shown in figure 8.8.

Figure 8.8: Trade Recorder showing all our positions for week 1

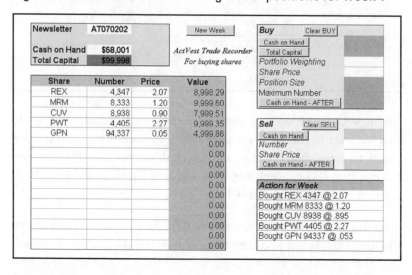

We've allocated about 42 per cent of our cash to these five positions and our total capital hasn't changed (we've just lost $2 because there's just been some rounding in the calculations).

That's a fairly busy week 1. Now it's time to save the Trade Recorder and move on to week 2! When we save week 1, the Trade Recorder retains only the information that we absolutely need to carry forward.

Week 2

Our Trade Recorder looks like figure 8.9 at the start of week 2. It shows only the information we need.

Figure 8.9: Trade Recorder at the start of week 2

Newsletter			New Week	
Cash on Hand	$58,001		*ActVest Trade Recorder*	
Total Capital			*For buying shares*	

Share	Number	Price	Value
CUV	8,938		0.00
GPN	94,337		0.00
MRM	8,333		0.00
PWT	4,405		0.00
REX	4,347		0.00
			0.00

The first thing to do this week is to check our stop losses. To do this we refer to the ActTrade data tables and see if any of our open positions have closed below the lower deviation. For this exercise I'm using an end-of-week stop loss, but in real time you would check your stop losses at the end of each day.

Stop losses checked! All our shares have had a weekly close above the lower deviation and they're all still in the data tables, meaning that their ROAR is above 80 per cent. If their ROAR was less than 80 per cent, they would simply be removed from the list. If this occurs, it is a stop loss condition where we have to immediately sell the share.

Now it's time to see if we can purchase any more shares because we still have cash to spend. We check the crossover charts and see that both the All Ords and the Small Ords are still crossed to the upside; that is, the grey line is above the black line at the right-hand edge of the chart (see figure 8.10).

Figure 8.10: crossover charts for All Ords and Small Ords, week 2

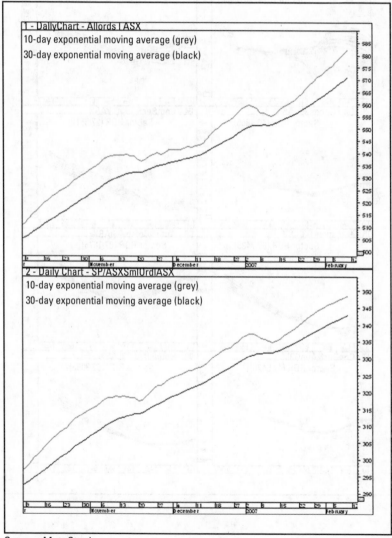

Source: MetaStock

The charts are still crossed to the upside, so the next thing to do is to check the sector MMA charts (see figure 8.11) and compile a list of the best rising sectors. Getting a feeling of *déjà vu*?

Figure 8.11: GICS industry group analysis charts

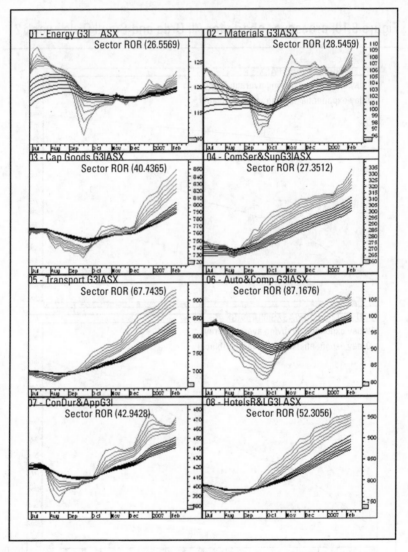

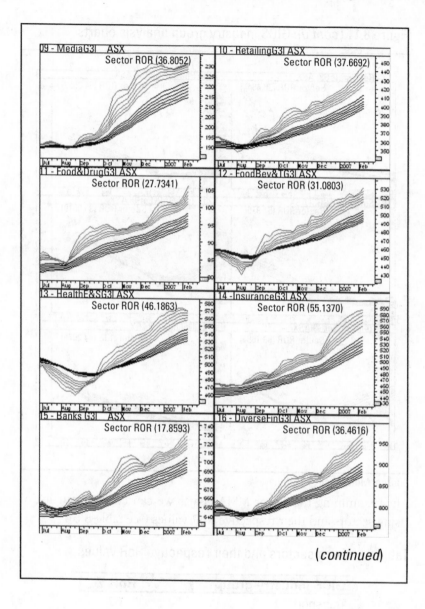

(*continued*)

Figure 8.11 (*cont'd*): GICS industry group analysis charts

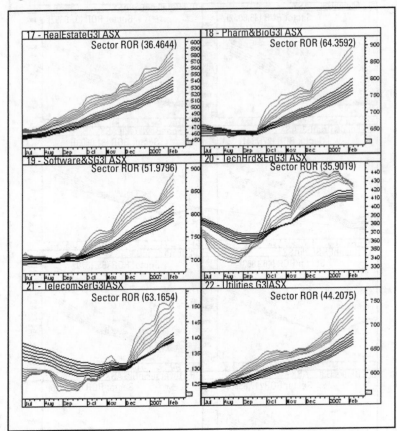

Source: MetaStock

After examining the sector MMA charts we can compile our list of rising sectors and their respective RoR values (see table 8.6).

Table 8.6: rising sectors and their respective RoR values

GICS industry group	RoR %
Transport	67
Pharm & biotech	64
Software & services	52
Utilities	44
Retailing	37
Diverse financials	36
Real estate	36
Food bev & tobacco	31

The only change here is the insurance sector. We've had a close look at its MMA chart and have decided to wait as the short-term moving averages have just started to roll over; only a little, but we will err on the side of caution in this case.

Looking at the share MMA charts we find that there are two candidates this week (see table 8.7).

Table 8.7: prospects showing entry criteria

Share	GICS industry group		ROAR %	Buy zone
MBA	Software & services	Up	190	in
SMY	Software & services	Dn	147	in

We'll knock out SMY; it hasn't met all our buy criteria because it has had a down week. We'll just stick with MBA now. Figure 8.12 shows us what MBA's MMA chart looks like and its values in the data table.

Figure 8.12: MBA's MMA chart and values in the data table

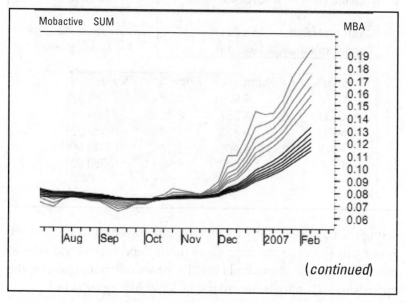

(*continued*)

Figure 8.12 (*cont'd*): MBA's MMA chart and values in the data table

Share code	Closing price ($)	Central cord ($)	Upper deviation ($)	Lower deviation ($)	ROAR (%)	Port. weighting for the 2% risk
MBA	0.205	0.231	0.278	0.153	190	6

Source: MetaStock

We can now add MBA to our portfolio. To do this we need to go back to the Trade Recorder. To work out our current total capital, we have to enter the current values of all our open positions and we'll use the closing price in the data tables for this exercise.

Our Trade Recorder currently looks like figure 8.13.

Figure 8.13: current Trade Recorder

Newsletter	AT070209		New Week
Cash on Hand	$58,001		*ActVest Trade Recorder*
Total Capital	$99,714		*For buying shares*

Share	Number	Price	Value
CUV	8,938	0.86	7,686.68
GPN	94,337	0.05	4,999.86
MRM	8,333	1.24	10,332.92
PWT	4,405	2.28	10,043.40
REX	4,347	1.99	8,650.53
			0.00

Using the buy calculator we can work out our position size and see how many shares to purchase. Once this is done, we can add MBA to our list of open positions and click the 'new week' button to save the spreadsheet. Our Trade Recorder now looks like figure 8.14.

At the end of week 2 we have six shares in our portfolio and approximately 50 per cent of our funds committed to the market. Now, on to week 3.

Figure 8.14: current view of our Trade Recorder

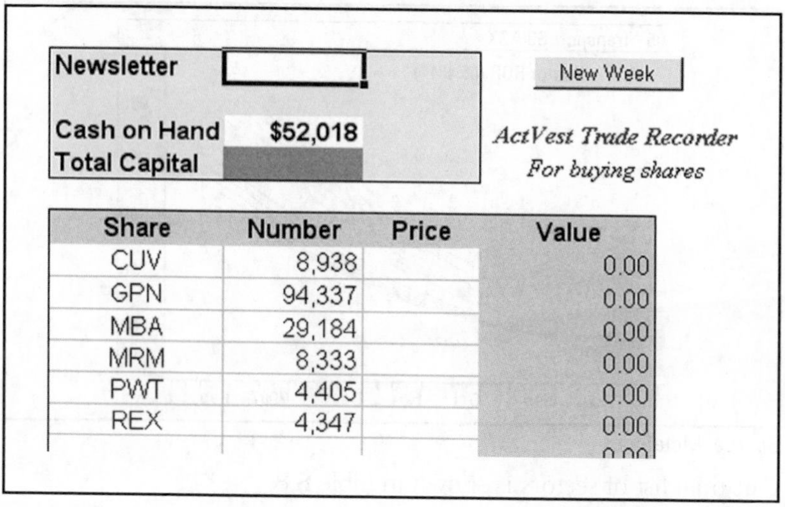

Newsletter				New Week	
Cash on Hand	**$52,018**			*ActVest Trade Recorder*	
Total Capital				*For buying shares*	

Share	Number	Price	Value
CUV	8,938		0.00
GPN	94,337		0.00
MBA	29,184		0.00
MRM	8,333		0.00
PWT	4,405		0.00
REX	4,347		0.00
			0.00

Week 3

First we check our stop losses. Again we'll make sure the weekly close is above the lower deviation and that the shares are still in the data tables, which means that their ROAR is greater than 80 per cent.

All our shares are above the lower deviation and are in the data tables, so our next step is to check the crossover charts again. Both the All Ords and the Small Ords are crossed to the upside so we can move onto the sectors.

We've narrowed down the sectors quite a bit further this week. Again we've been tough on the MMA charts and this time we've ruled out the transport, real estate, pharm & biotech and utilities sectors because the short-term moving averages are showing some early signs of weakness. The MMA chart of the transport sector is shown in figure 8.15. The short-term moving averages are starting to roll over just a little.

Figure 8.15: MMA chart of the transport sector

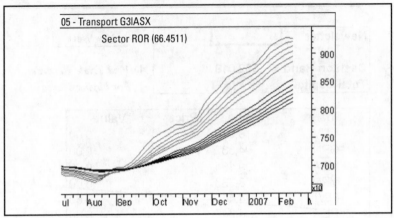

Source: MetaStock

Our final list of sectors is shown in table 8.8.

Table 8.8: final list of sectors

GICS industry group	ROR %
Software & services	52
Retailing	40
Diverse financials	37
Food bev & tobacco	31

Once we've gone through the share MMA charts, we're left with SMY (figure 8.16).

Figure 8.16: SMY's MMA chart and details of SMY

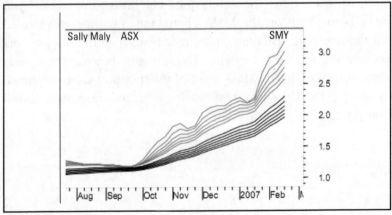

Source: MetaStock

Share	GICS Industry Group		ROAR %	Buy zone
SMY	Software & services	Up	146	in

SMY's entry in the data table is shown in table 8.9.

Table 8.9: SMY's entry in the data table

Share code	Closing price ($)	Central cord ($)	Upper deviation ($)	Lower deviation ($)	ROAR (%)	Port. weighting for the 2% risk
SMY	3.390	3.666	4.244	2.731	146	9

Time to update the Trade Recorder with the values of our open positions so we can work out our total capital, then buy SMY. After we've added SMY and before we've cleared the buy calculator our Trade Recorder looks like figure 8.17.

Figure 8.17: our Trade Recorder after we've added SMY and before we've cleared the buy calculator

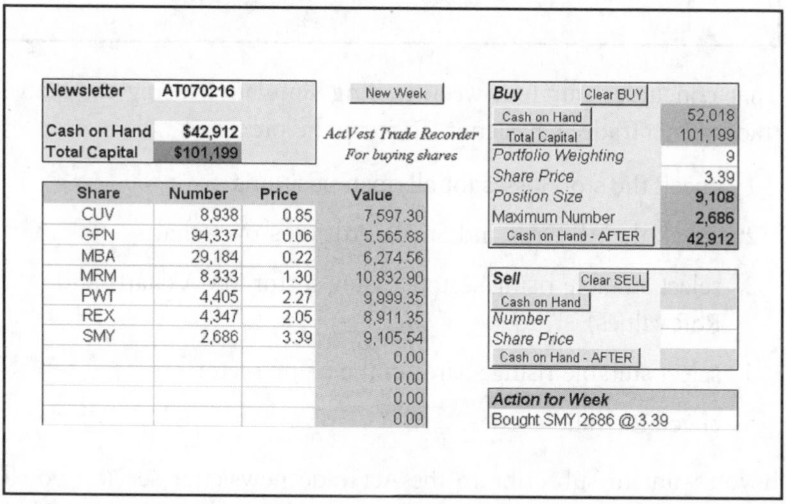

That's the end of week 3. We have seven shares in our portfolio and nearly 58 per cent of our capital allocated to the market. By now you should be getting a good idea of what it's like to use the active trading strategy with the ActVest Trade Recorder.

Week 4

This week we'll check our stop losses, then look at the final value of our portfolio.

We've checked our stop losses and all our shares are still above the lower deviation and in the data tables. Next, we'll use the weekly closing prices from the data tables to work out the value of our portfolio in the Trade Recorder (see figure 8.18).

Figure 8.18: value of our portfolio

Newsletter	AT070223		New Week
Cash on Hand	$42,912		*ActVest Trade Recorder*
Total Capital	$102,802		*For buying shares*

Share	Number	Price	Value
CUV	8,938	0.98	8,759.24
GPN	94,337	0.06	5,282.87
MBA	29,184	0.19	5,399.04
MRM	8,333	1.27	10,582.91
PWT	4,405	2.28	10,043.40
REX	4,347	2.07	8,998.29
SMY	2,686	4.03	10,824.58
			0.00

That concludes our four-week trading simulation using the active trading (ActTrade) newsletter. To recap the process:

1 check the stop losses for all open positions

2 check the All Ords and Small Ords crossover charts

3 select suitable rising sectors (using sector MMA charts and RoR values)

4 select suitable rising shares in the rising sectors

5 check for valid entries.

If you want to subscribe to the ActTrade newsletter service, you'll find a subscription form near the back of this book. As an added bonus, if you subscribe to the ActTrade newsletter using the form in this book, you'll receive a free copy of the ActVest Trade Recorder.

Now it's on to part III, where Alan introduces you to breakout trading.

PART III
Break out trading

Chapter 9
Introduction to breakout trading

In the last few chapters we discussed a trend trading strategy I call active trading. Trend trading is a very powerful way to trade, except when the market isn't trending. Sometimes the market goes sideways rather than up or down. The chart in figure 9.1, of the Australian All Ordinaries index, illustrates this. In the second half of the chart you can see the market went nowhere in a hurry—except sideways.

Figure 9.1: All Ordinaries index weekly chart

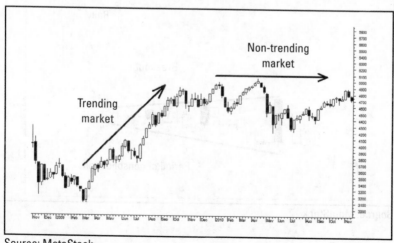

Source: MetaStock

I love trend trading and I think it's the most bulletproof approach to trading shares. It's simple to understand and relatively easy to do. But, sadly, sometimes market conditions simply aren't suited to trend trading. Rather than sit on my hands during sideways conditions, I turn to an entirely different strategy: breakout trading.

Breakout trading is quite different to trend trading, so prepare yourself to think differently. In this chapter we approach the business of share trading from a very different perspective. Let's begin with a very succinct definition of what breakout trading is:

> *Breakout trading is about identifying breakouts after periods of price consolidation, then exploiting the rallies that follow for profit.*

We will discuss each part of this definition throughout this chapter. In basic terms it means we look for a breakout (a significant price jump) from a period of consolidation and buy into the rally that follows. Figure 9.2 is an example of a breakout pattern that we would look for. Note the price rally that followed the breakout.

Figure 9.2: a period of consolidation followed by a breakout and ensuing price rally

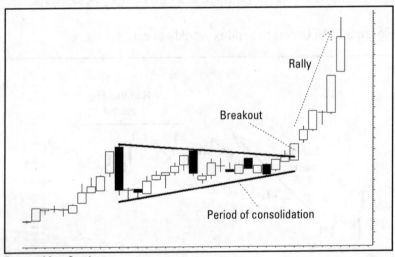

Source: MetaStock

This sort of trading operates well in a non-trending market, primarily because we don't have to wait for weeks of price activity to confirm our moment of entry. Rather, it uses a price pattern for the entry signal, then a very sensitive momentum-based indicator for the exit. Throughout this chapter we will explore details of these signals, including why they occur and how they can be incorporated into a trading strategy.

Breakout trading is a very agile or nimble form of trading. It's very effective when the market is sideways, so it dovetails well with trend trading strategies such as active trading. By combining trend trading with breakout trading it's possible to produce trading opportunities throughout virtually all market conditions.

The entry—the breakout pattern

The first thing you'll notice about the period of consolidation is that it looks like a triangle resting on its side, and that's pretty much what it is. Now let's be a bit more specific about the entry signal and its characteristics so that we can identify entries as they come along.

Essentially there are two parts to the pattern. The first part is the period of consolidation, or the triangle. This is the precursor to the actual breakout and is often referred to as the trade set up. The entry trigger is the breakout from this triangle. This will usually be a single candle that is strong-looking and that closes outside the boundaries of the preceding triangle.

It is due to this single candle entry trigger that the tempo of breakout trading is very different from trend trading. In breakout trading we enter the trade the moment the breakout occurs. The chart in figure 9.3 (overleaf) shows the two parts of the breakout pattern: the period of consolidation followed by the breakout candle.

Think back to our discussion about trend trading in chapter 6. There, we were looking for an established trend with at least two to three months of rising price action. Waiting for trend confirmation is an integral part of trend trading and greatly improves the probability of success. Breakout trading is different.

135

Figure 9.3: the period of consolidation (the set up) and the breakout candle (the trigger)

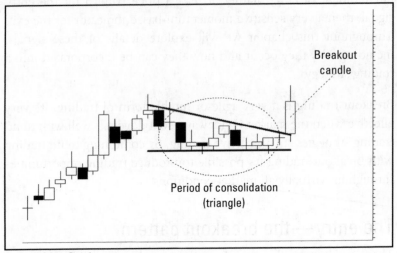

Source: MetaStock

With breakout trading we act on the single breakout candle. This is a nimble strategy, but the breakout candle must be preceded by a period of narrowing consolidation that should be relatively easy to identify. If this is the case then our chances of success and the probability that a price rally will occur are very good. Breakout trading relies on price consolidation, so let's explore the reasons behind this.

Points of agreement

During a period of consolation, price activity gradually narrows into what we call a 'point of agreement' (POA). If you consider the consolidation pattern in figure 9.4, you can see how the price activity is spiralling in towards a point. At this point near the tip of the triangle, when the market is almost still, market participants seem to be content to neither buy nor sell the share. They are essentially agreeing that the price the share is trading at is fair value by refraining from buying or selling it. It appears the share is no longer a bargain for those who want to buy it, nor is it selling at a high enough premium for those who want to dispose of it.

Figure 9.4: the point of agreement is at the tip of the triangle, just before the breakout

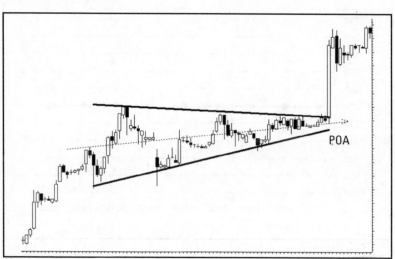

POA

Source: MetaStock

You'll also note in figure 9.4 that there is a line running along the middle of the triangle. This line identifies the midpoint of the share's trading range throughout the period of consolidation. In contrast to the POA, which occurs at the tip of the triangle, this line is effectively the 'line of agreement'. It points towards the POA, which is often not actually reached by the price.

If a market remained at a POA indefinitely then the market would cease to exist. Markets must constantly move in order to survive. If everyone agreed on the value or future value of a share, its price would stagnate and eventually the market would dry up and finally dwindle into non-existence. This would be the case for the $50 note, if anyone was ever silly enough to try to trade in $50 notes.

Not many people would be willing to buy a $50 note for $60; nor would many people sell one for $40. This is because we all agree a $50 note has a value of $50 (see figure 9.5, overleaf). Therefore, there is no market for $50 notes. The same goes for shares. It is our disagreement about their value that drives the price up and down. Therefore, any period of agreement in the market is only ever temporary.

Figure 9.5: imaginary price chart of a $50 note

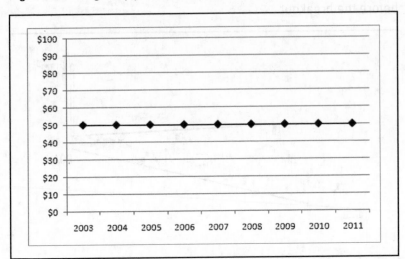

A period of consolidation can't persist. The market will eventually break out, either up or down, because something will inevitably happen to stimulate it into action. Markets revel in news and can react to anything from rumours to speculation, so it's not surprising that the price inevitably finds a reason to rally and breakout.

Here's another way of visualising it: imagine the natural weather phenomenon known as the calm before the storm. This is when an eerie silence takes hold with little or no wind and there are black clouds on the horizon. My experience with breakout patterns is that the consolidation phase is very much like a calm moment before a storm. When the breakout finally happens it can be quite dramatic.

The exit from a breakout trade

I hope you're getting the feel for what breakout trading is all about: catching the rally after a POA. This strategy is not about buying into a stable ongoing trend, but the nimble exploitation of a rally after a breakout pattern occurs. Therefore, we need an agile exit strategy to lock in profits quickly.

Some rallies can be quite short, but others can last for a considerable length of time. In either circumstance, the best way to manage a breakout trade is with momentum because it gives a timely indication of when the initial breakout rally is slowing. I prefer to use the moving average convergence divergence (MACD) indicator to measure momentum, and generally I'm quite happy to use the default settings. I discussed the MACD indicator in chapter 3 and it is available in virtually all modern charting software programs.

However, the way I use the MACD indicator in breakout trading does differ from its commonly accepted use, which employs crossover signals for entry and exit (see chapter 3). Instead, I concentrate on the direction of the MACD line. When I'm in a breakout rally going up, I stay in the trade while the MACD line is rising. But when it turns down it indicates that the momentum is slowing, so I immediately exit the trade.

Figure 9.6 shows a breakout trade with the MACD indicator at the top of the chart. The thick black line is the MACD line. When the MACD line starts to fall it signals an exit from the breakout trade. The thinner line is the MACD's signal line, but I'm only interested in the MACD line for this application.

Figure 9.6: MACD as a momentum indicator

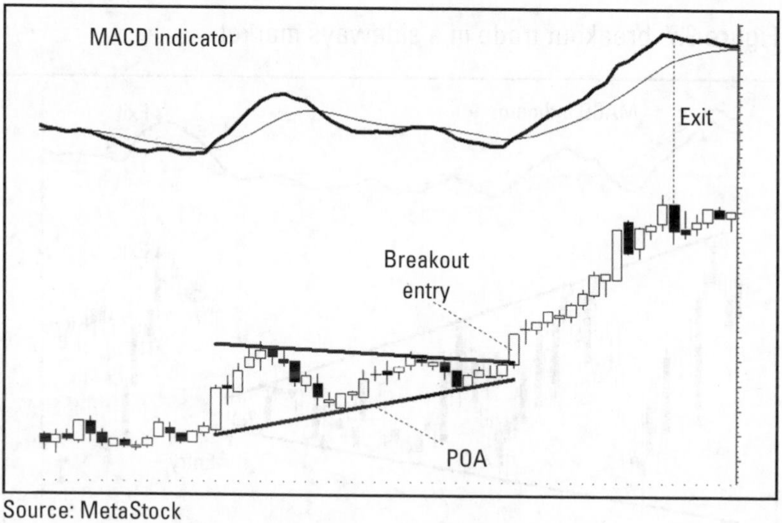

Source: MetaStock

In the chart you can see how the momentum and therefore the MACD line rose as the rally ran, but fell when the rally had finished. This is a very different way to exit a market compared to trend trading, which generally relies on a price-related trigger as a stop loss. This makes complete sense as acting on a not-so-sensitive, price-related stop loss is appropriate when trend trading because there needs to be some allowance for volatility and normal price pull backs to occur.

But in breakout trading, we want the volatility to be in one direction only: the direction of the rally. Any significant volatility or movement against the rally suggests that the initial rally may be coming to an end. Momentum reacts quickly and will soon warn us if the rally is beginning to falter. This is what we want for breakout trading: to trade only the breakout rally and exit as soon as it finishes.

A good way to illustrate the dexterity of the MACD momentum exit is with figure 9.7. Here is a breakout trade in what is essentially a non-trending, sideways market. No significant trend developed here at all, yet there was a clear POA with a strong breakout. The momentum indicator signalled a timely exit, which captured a profit.

Figure 9.7: breakout trade in a sideways market

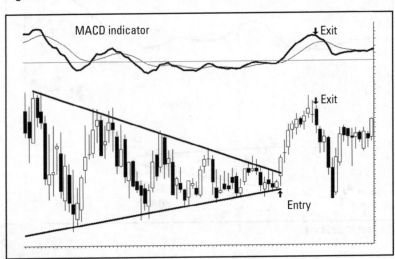

Source: MetaStock

Breakout trading in a trending market

Here's a bonus: breakout trading also works in a trending market. Breakout patterns can occur during a trend as well as at other times. The chart in figure 9.8 shows two breakout trades that occurred within a trending environment. What's more, the two breakout trades took a reasonable chunk of the available profit in the trend as well.

Figure 9.8: breakout trades in a trend

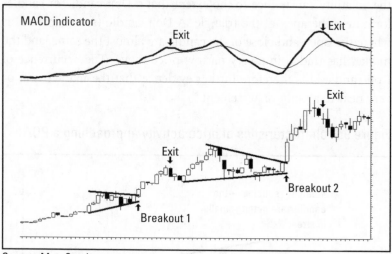

Source: MetaStock

While I prefer to trend trade if I am confident that a trend exists, sometimes it may not be clear if there is a trend, particularly at the beginning of one. This is where breakout trading is a particularly handy addition to trend trading because it can get you into trades much earlier.

Identifying a breakout pattern

Now that we've covered the strategy overview, let's look at some of the details of the strategy.

Recognising a breakout pattern can take a bit of practise, so here are some guidelines that will help you with the process. Remember that any pattern in share trading is a bit like a snowflake—each one is different, but they all have common elements.

The common characteristics to expect in a breakout pattern are universal. Remember when we were talking about POAs earlier on and it appeared that when the market participants were agreeing, the price activity was largely still? This means the price activity will narrow towards a point, forming a triangle, volatility will reduce and sometimes the volume will reduce as well.

The chart in figure 9.9 shows some of these characteristics. Sometimes the volatility can reduce to the extent that a Doji candle or candles form near the apex of the triangle. A Doji candle (see chapter 2) is where the open and close of the candle are almost the same, and the market has traded in a very narrow price range. The occurrence of Doji candle(s) is therefore further evidence that the market is at or very near to a point of agreement.

Figure 9.9: characteristics of price activity approaching a POA

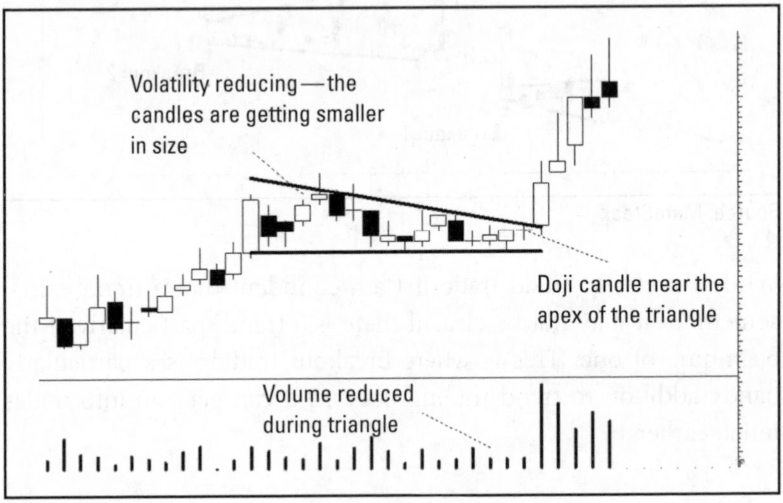

Source: MetaStock

Most people will 'see' the triangle in a chart before they even attempt to put the converging trend lines on the chart. This is good because it means the pattern is probably quite clear and the converging trend lines are simply confirming the obvious.

Another feature of price activity during the period of consolidation is that, within the triangle, the price waves should be getting smaller and smaller, along with the size of the candles. These are a general measure of volatility, which we would expect to reduce if investors and traders are becoming less interested in buying and selling.

Another characteristic to look for is a reduction in volume (the number of shares traded) approaching the POA. However, volume does not always support a valid breakout pattern. Sometimes there can be no change in volume even if a POA and breakout rally occur. Therefore, I look for volume confirmation, but I don't rely on it if everything else looks good; volume is a secondary form of analysis.

The characteristics of price approaching a POA are:

- price narrows within converging trend lines (triangle shaped)
- volatility reduces
- Doji candle may be present at the tip of the POA
- volume may be low approaching the POA.

Identifying a breakout candle

Breakout candles have certain characteristics too, and it should be no surprise that they are pretty much the opposite of the characteristics that develop approaching a POA. After all, the breakout candle is indicating a reversal in the market dynamic, from a complete lack of volatility to an aggressive shift or jump in price.

We therefore expect the breakout candle to close outside the boundaries of the triangle. We also expect the volatility to increase, so the size of the breakout candle should be larger than those immediately preceding it. Sometimes the volume will also increase, although, again, this is not always the case.

Figure 9.10 (overleaf) highlights these characteristics in a breakout candle. We want to see a change in personality; a sign that the moment of the POA has well and truly passed.

Figure 9.10: characteristics of a breakout candle

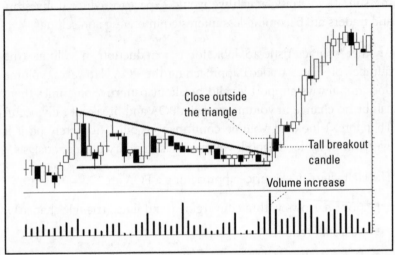

Source: MetaStock

A breakout candle has the following characteristics:

- it closes outside the boundaries of the triangle
- it is tall, with its close near its high
- volume may be strong on the breakout.

Short selling with breakout trading

Breakouts can occur downwards as well as upwards. This means that it is best not to pre-empt a breakout, but to wait for it to occur before entering a trade. Of course we can trade breakouts that occur to the downside and breakout trading is probably the most successful method of trading falling markets that I know of. This is because when markets move downwards, price activity tends to fall aggressively, rallying rather than trending.

To trade a breakout to the downside, all we have to do is flip our strategy upside down to produce trades for short selling. Short selling is not widely practiced in Australia and there aren't a lot of derivatives available for short selling. However, as I tend to stick to the ASX300 index's constituent shares for breakout trading (more on this shortly), CFDs are available for many of these equities.

Figure 9.11 shows an example of a breakout to the down side. Note how the MACD line is falling during the downward rally. Here the momentum is tracked in the downward direction and the exit signal is given when the MACD line turns up.

Figure 9.11: breakout trade to the down side

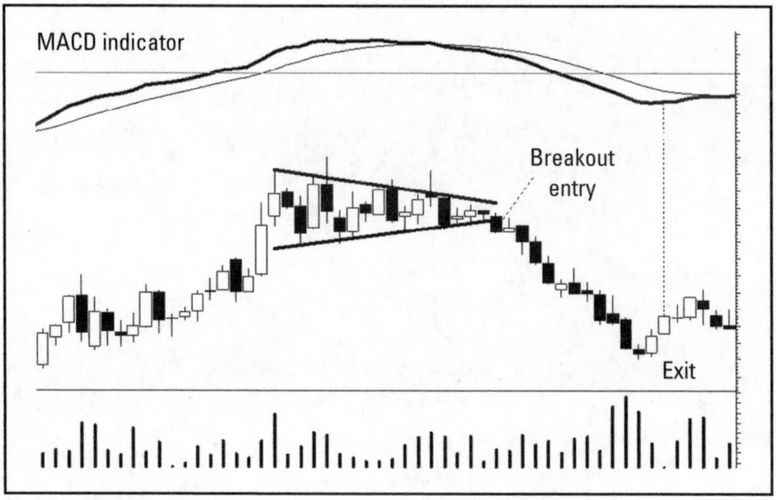

Source: MetaStock

The stock market isn't symmetrical in behaviour and has a greater tendency to rise than fall, so the majority of breakouts are to the up side. Short selling can be overlooked, depending on a trader's preference.

In this chapter, we've developed a behavioural understanding of the breakout pattern and introduced some of the essential components of my breakout trading strategy. Now we'll start to drill down into the specifics by taking a closer look at my complete breakout trading toolbox.

Chapter 10
Tools for breakout trading

In this chapter we discuss the details of the tools and indicators used in my breakout trading strategy. Many of these tools are quantitative and can be mechanised with a charting program. However, a few are qualitative, such as trend lines, which cannot be easily mechanised.

As with trend trading using the active trading strategy, I consider it an advantage to have a mix of qualitative and quantitative measures in a strategy. This means we can let a computer carry out the simple but laborious tasks, while the human brain carries out the more intricate analysis of pattern recognition, where some allowance for natural variation is required.

Of course, it is not a good idea to entirely trust ourselves with the final decisions when trading, so it pays to have the qualitative measures near the beginning of the process and let the mechanical measures give the final go ahead.

This is the approach I use in trend trading with both active trading and breakout trading, where the qualitative measures are used in the search and filtering process to find the trading opportunities, but the actual entry trigger, position sizing and exit signals are predominantly mechanical. In this chapter I've highlighted whether each stage of the process is quantitative or qualitative.

Furthermore, I believe it is important that traders are aware of how much emphasis a strategy places on discretion, because some of us prefer more discretionary input while others prefer to exercise less discretion.

Let's look at some of the individual components in the breakout trading strategy.

Points of agreement (qualitative)

The shape of a consolidation pattern in the lead up to a point of agreement will always be triangular. However, triangles do come in various shapes and sizes. There are ascending, descending, equilateral and wedge-shaped triangles. This is one instance where the human eye will recognise the pattern faster and more reliably than a computer.

Figure 10.1 shows some examples of various triangles that you may come across. The critical feature is that they narrow in towards a point and you must be able to define them with converging trend lines. Of course, a clearly defined triangle means a clearly defined point of agreement.

Figure 10.1: examples of various triangles you may come across in consolidation patterns

Ascending triangle

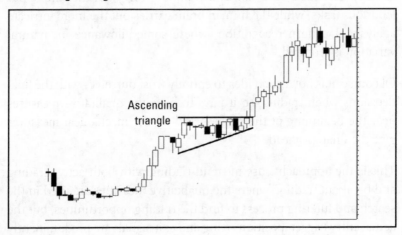

Descending triangle

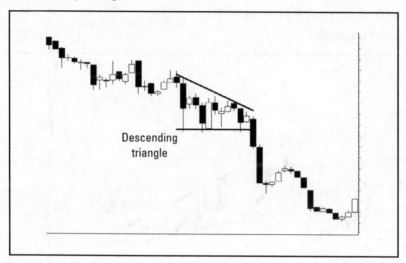

Descending
triangle

Equilateral triangle

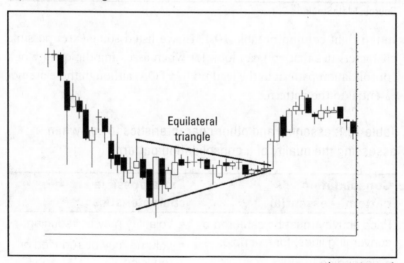

Equilateral
triangle

(*continued*)

Figure 10.1 (*cont'd*): examples of various triangles you may come across in consolidation patterns

Falling wedge

Source: MetaStock

In the right column of table 10.1, I have listed some extra possible characteristics that you can look for when assessing the quality of a consolidation pattern in the lead up to a POA, although these are not essential to the pattern.

Table 10.1: essential and other characteristics to use when assessing the quality of a consolidation pattern

Consolidation pattern — essential	Extra possible characteristics
Price activity must be captured by converging lines, for example: • ascending triangle • descending triangle • equilateral triangle • rising wedge • falling wedge.	• Volatility may be reducing. • Volume may be reduced or reducing. • Doji candle(s) may be present prior to the breakout.

Consolidation patterns and the subsequent points of agreement are often visible to the human eye without trend lines; adding the trend lines confirms what you are already seeing in the chart. If you have your own charting software then I recommend you give it a try. You'll be surprised how easy these patterns can be to spot, even at first glance.

While I covered this in chapter 2, a quick review of the critical points on the construction of triangles won't hurt. When circumscribing a triangle the trend lines must enclose all the real bodies in the price pattern; in other words, never draw through a real body of a candle.

However, you can choose to sit trend lines on the real bodies or slightly wider, on the shadows of the candles. In the charts of triangles in figure 10.1, you will see a mixture of lines sitting on shadows and real bodies. The important point is that all the real bodies are included and the price is narrowing in towards a point; that is, the trend lines must be converging.

Pivot points (qualitative and quantitative)

Price action moves in waves and pivot points are the high and low turning points of these waves. Our primary interest in these high and low turning points is the identification of the last pivot point in the direction of the breakout, as a reference for the breakout candle. This is because, for the breakout candle to be significant, it must not only break out of the triangle, but it must also make a new high (or low) by moving beyond the previous pivot point.

This is probably best explained with a working example, so in figure 10.2 (overleaf) I have highlighted the pivot points within a consolidation pattern. There are a couple of pivot point highs and a couple of pivot point lows.

The breakout is to the upside, so the pivot point that we need to reference is the pivot point high just prior to the breakout. We are looking for the breakout candle to close above this pivot point. I have highlighted the appropriate pivot point in the chart in figure 10.3 (overleaf), along with the breakout candle.

Figure 10.2: pivot points in a consolidation pattern

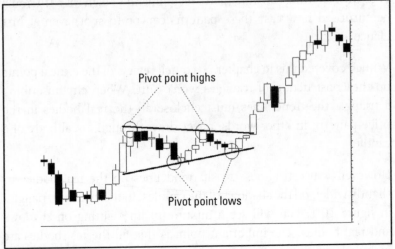

Source: MetaStock

Figure 10.3: breakout candle closes above previous pivot point high

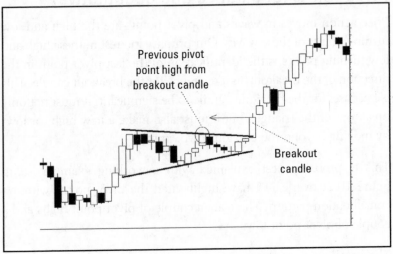

Source: MetaStock

The opposite applies for breakouts to the downside; the close of the breakout candle has to close below the previous pivot point low. While it is a mechanical process to determine whether or not the breakout candle has eclipsed the previous pivot point, the identification of the previous pivot point is discretionary.

Breakout candles (qualitative and quantitative)

The breakout candle is the most critical component in breakout trading because it is the signal for us to take action. It signifies the change in sentiment from calm to stormy or, if you prefer, from agreement to disagreement, and is therefore a cornerstone of the strategy.

We therefore need to be very particular about what we consider to be a breakout candle, so there are quite a few criteria to assess when it comes to identifying them. The first few criteria for a breakout candle up are:

- the breakout candle is preceded by a period of consolidation
- it must close outside the triangle
- the close is above the previous pivot point high.

For a breakout candle down the first few criteria are:

- the breakout candle is preceded by a period of consolidation
- it must close outside the triangle
- the close is below the previous pivot point low.

We covered these criteria while talking about consolidation patterns, triangles, points of agreement and pivot points. These are qualitative measures and therefore need to be assessed by eye in the charts. But a breakout candle needs to have several more attributes as well.

The nature of a breakout candle is to have increased volatility, with a close near its high (for a breakout to the upside). A breakout candle can be assessed by eye by looking for a tall candle with a close near its high, or you can be more specific and measure these mathematically using the following criteria. I have included some MetaStock coding for these measures in appendix B.

Volatility measure = a breakout candle to the upside must close above the candle immediately preceding it by more than half the ATR (17)

Closing position = a breakout candle to the upside must close above its midpoint

ATR (17) stands for average true range with a period of 17. Average true range is a measure of volatility (see chapter 3). The use of a period of 17 is suggested here because recent backtesting that I've done indicates this is the average length of a triangle. This is relevant because a breakout candle's volatility will be relative to the average volatility of the preceding triangle or consolidation period.

The other specified elements mentioned in the above mathematical benchmarks to measure volatility have also been selected based on recent backtesting. Of course these elements can be adjusted if you're an experienced trader and inclined to tinker with such things, but I do recommend sufficient backtesting to ensure they give the results you're looking for.

Finally, two more criteria are needed. The first is to ensure the MACD line is above its signal line and rising (assuming you're trading a breakout to the upside). This is to ensure momentum is behind the rally that has begun.

The second is that the closing price must be above 20 cents; a sensible measure to ensure there is sufficient liquidity by avoiding trading microcapitalisation (microcap) shares. Again, both of these can be assessed by eye or with mathematical modelling.

MACD measure = a breakout to the upside must have the MACD line above its signal line and rising

Closing price = a breakout candle to the upside must close above 20 cents to help ensure there is sufficient liquidity

All of these criteria are summarised in table 10.2. I have also included the criteria needed for a breakout candle to the downside for short selling. These are generally the opposite of the requirements for a breakout to the upside except for the last criteria concerning liquidity. For breakouts to the downside it makes more sense to limit the price of shares to those above $1 because those below $1 will not have far to go before they hit zero.

A candle needs to pass seven criteria before it can be considered a breakout candle. The chart in figure 10.4 shows a valid breakout candle with some of the criteria highlighted.

Table 10.2: essential characteristics for a breakout candle

Breakout candle — up	Breakout candle — down
• breakout candle is preceded by a POA	• breakout candle is preceded by a POA
• it must close outside the triangle	• it must close outside the triangle
• the close is above the previous pivot point high	• the close is below the previous pivot point low
• the close is above the previous candle by more than half the ATR (17)	• the close is below the previous candle by more than half the ATR (17)
• closes above its midpoint	• the close is below its midpoint
• the MACD line is above its signal line and rising	• the MACD line is below its signal line and falling
• the close is greater than 20 cents to help ensure there is sufficient liquidity.	• the close is greater than $1 to help ensure there is room above zero for the price to continue falling for a reasonable period.

Figure 10.4: valid breakout candle

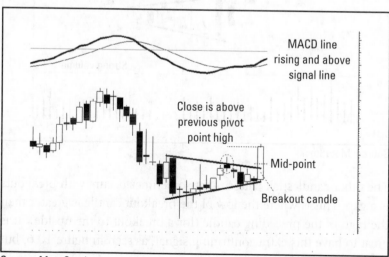

Source: MetaStock

The breakout candle is a critical component of any breakout trading strategy. In my *Breakout trading* newsletter only those shares that pass all the above criteria are included as possible trading opportunities. We examine this further when we put the strategy to the test.

Extra guidelines for breakout candles (qualitative)

What hasn't been included in the above discussion is a volume measure. As with POA, volume confirmation is one of those things that is nice to have in a breakout pattern, but isn't essential. Breakouts can occur without necessarily being accompanied by strong volume and therefore I regard rising volume as a guideline rather than a rule. The chart in figure 10.5 shows a valid breakout that is accompanied by strong, rising volume. The same goes for candlestick patterns such as a Doji in the apex of a POA; it's nice to have as an extra signal but it's not essential.

Figure 10.5: breakout with strong volume

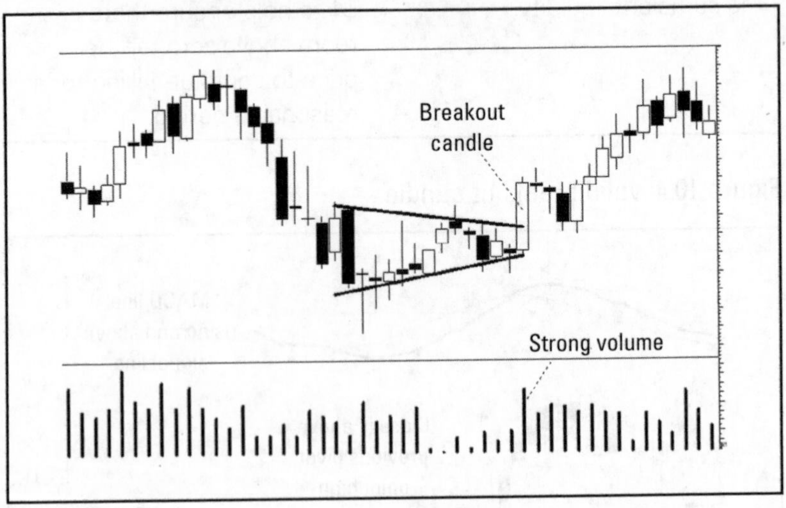

Source: MetaStock

The other candlestick pattern that sometimes occurs with breakouts is a gap. This is where the low of the breakout candle is greater than the high of the preceding candle (for a breakout to the upside). It is great to have this extra confirming signal, as seen in figure 10.6, but it is not absolutely necessary.

Figure 10.6: gap preceding a breakout candle

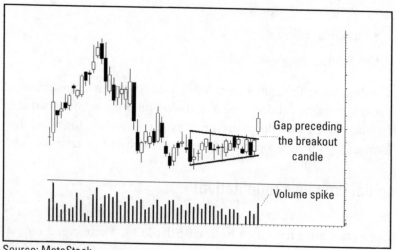

Source: MetaStock

I tend to use the following extra guidelines for a breakout candle (up and down) as a means for selecting between breakout trades if I have plenty to choose from:

- there is strong volume with the breakout candle compared to the volume at the point of agreement
- there is a gap between the breakout candle and the preceding candle
- there is a Doji candle near the apex of the POA prior to the breakout candle.

Price-related stop loss (qualitative and quantitative)

As well as the MACD indicator's momentum-based exit signal, which we looked at in chapter 9, it is also necessary to have a price-related stop loss. This additional stop loss fulfils several key functions. Firstly it is used for risk management purposes, which in turn regulates our position sizing. Secondly, it will test to see if the POA remains valid, giving an exit signal if it fails. And finally, it will follow closely behind the price rally as a trailing stop loss for extra safety.

In all trading there are risks, and as traders we need to be aware of them and plan for all eventualities. In breakout trading, a price-related stop loss can help us with this. It is made up of two parts, with two functions:

- an initial stop loss
- a trailing stop loss.

The first part, the initial stop loss, tests to see that the breakout pattern remains valid during the trade while the second part, the trailing stop loss, follows the price as it progresses. Together, they form a stop loss that I like to represent on a chart as a series of dots.

Initial stop loss (qualitative)

Breakout patterns can fail at the outset and, when they do, it usually means the price has fallen back past the POA. Therefore, an initial stop loss can be placed at the point of agreement so if the price falls past this level it indicates an exit condition. The determination of exactly where the POA lies is a qualitative exercise.

Drawing a mid-line through the triangle (that is, a line of agreement) will give a reasonably accurate indication of where the absolute or precise POA would theoretically lie. Therefore, we can place the initial stop loss or POA stop loss on this line at the point where the breakout has occurred (see figure 10.7).

Figure 10.7: placement of the initial stop loss on the line of agreement

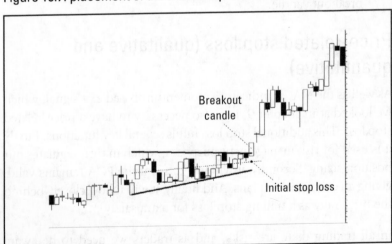

Source: MetaStock

158

Trailing stop loss (quantitative)

The trailing stop loss part uses the chandelier approach as I described in chapter 3. As the name suggests, a chandelier stop loss hangs down from the highest high of the trade (for a long trade) by a set displacement (see figure 10.8). This method is used because it is instantly reactive to any advance in price, which is necessary when trading a strong rally.

Figure 10.8: initial stop loss and trailing stop loss

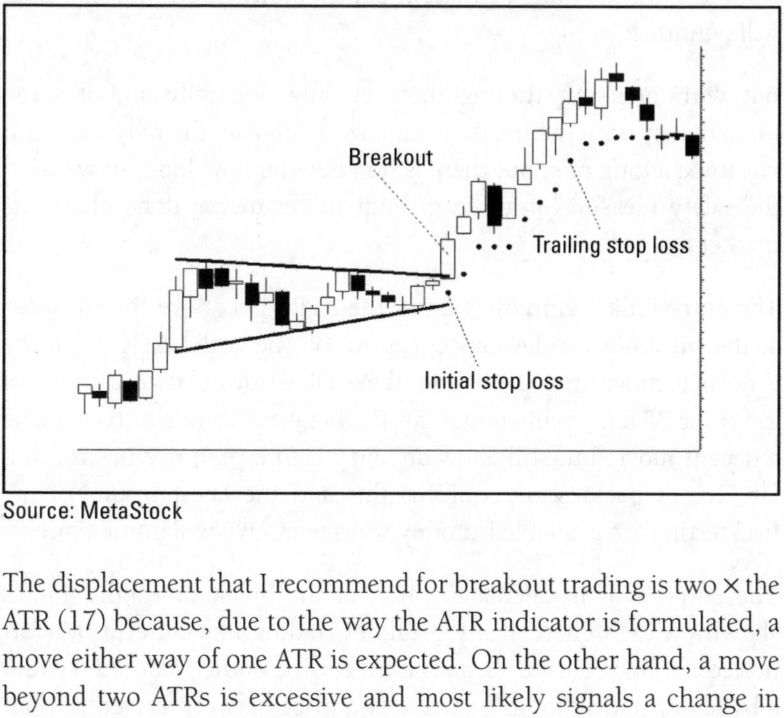

Source: MetaStock

The displacement that I recommend for breakout trading is two × the ATR (17) because, due to the way the ATR indicator is formulated, a move either way of one ATR is expected. On the other hand, a move beyond two ATRs is excessive and most likely signals a change in market direction—and sentiment.

By employing these two price-related stop losses along with the MACD momentum stop loss, we aren't going to be hanging around if the market moves against us. What's more, now that we have an initial stop loss price, we can work out our position size according to the 2 per cent risk rule.

There's one more critical parameter that we need to complete our toolbox.

Entry limit (quantitative)

Breakouts can be dramatic and this is a good thing, but since we don't enter the market until after the breakout has begun, it may simply move too far before we can actually enter the trade. There comes a point when the risk begins to outweigh the possible reward, so there needs to be a limit to how far we will pursue a trade.

Remember that breakout trading is different from trend trading. In trend trading it is possible to jump onboard during any minor dip along the way, so long as there is some confirmation that the trend will continue.

But with breakout trading there is only one rally and it starts immediately with the breakout candle. Of course, the rally may turn out to be a long one, but there is no knowing how long, so we need the safety measure of an entry limit to ensure we don't chase the market too far.

The entry limit I employ is 2.5 × the ATR (17) above the stop loss at the breakout candle. Since a move of one × the ATR would be a normal move, based on how the ATR is formulated, a move of 2.5 × the ATR is room enough for the breakout candle to have made a decent move, but still allow an entry before the price has run too far. Recent backtesting confirms this and the latest results of my backtesting are available from my website at <www.alanhull.com>.

The entry limit is calculated once, at the breakout candle and is shown on each chart in my breakout trading newsletter as a short horizontal line. This level stays fixed for the entire trade. Entry into a breakout trade should be made at a price between the entry limit and the stop loss, typically during the trading period immediately following the breakout candle (see figure 10.9).

Figure 10.9: breakout trade with entry limit

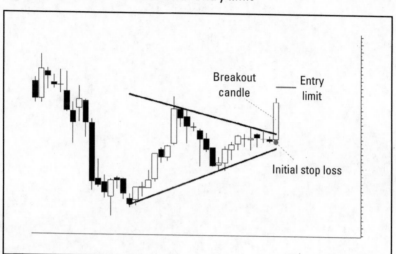

Source: MetaStock

In the next chapter, we will look at a step-by-step guide to breakout trading as it would be performed.

Chapter 11
Applying the breakout trading strategy

We're at the stage where we can bring together all the components of the breakout trading strategy and put them into a trading plan. For the trading plan we'll use the same framework we used for the active investing strategy in chapter 5.

You will find, however, that some parts of the trading plan that were important for trend trading are not so relevant when it comes to breakout trading. As we work through the steps of the plan we will execute an example trade to illustrate the process.

Premise

This is the easy bit: breakout trading is a short-term, medium risk strategy that identifies breakouts from periods of consolidation and exploits price momentum in the rallies that follow. Breakouts from periods of consolidation can occur in any market condition, so the breakout trading strategy is suitable to use when the market is going sideways or trending in either direction.

Broad market assessment

When trend trading, it is very important to assess the general market conditions and ensure that they are suitable for trend trading. This greatly improves the probability of success with trend trading, whereas breakout trading performs well in sideways conditions and trending conditions. No broad market assessment is therefore required for breakout trading because it can be applied to the market at virtually any time.

Fundamental analysis

When there is a breakout there could be a tangible reason or reasons behind it. However, the strategy presented here is concerned with reacting to price behaviour rather than predicting or analysing the reasons why it happened. Fundamental analysis is therefore something that can be bypassed completely when breakout trading.

You may still be tempted to sneak a look at fundamental information when breakout trading. But the short-term nature of this system means the trades are generally well within the time frame of most formal company reporting so that it becomes unrealistic to use half yearly or annual data effectively.

Search procedure

Any search procedure needs to start with a universe of shares. With active trading, small to midcap shares generally produced the aggressive trends we wanted; therefore, it made sense to scan the entire market for that strategy.

With breakout trading it is the same situation, where most shares will show evidence of breakout patterns regardless of the size of the company. I have noticed, however, that it is generally the small to midcap shares that produce the lengthier rallies following a point of agreement (POA). Therefore, the entire market can be scanned, with the possible exclusion of larger blue chip shares.

I often conduct my searches by eyeballing each chart; therefore, I limit myself to the top 300. It doesn't take too long to flick through them all each week because I know exactly what I'm looking for. Eyeballing the charts also means I get to know them well and can sometimes see developing POAs, which is useful.

What I am looking for is a breakout candle following a consolidation pattern and point of agreement. The chart in figure 11.1 shows the sort of share I would select.

Figure 11.1: possible breakout trading opportunity

Source: MetaStock

The chart in figure 11.2 (overleaf) shows the same share marked with trend lines to highlight the consolidation pattern. These trading opportunities are reasonably obvious when you know what you are looking for.

Breakouts can occur from price patterns other than from POAs, such as from a channel or a head and shoulders pattern. These breakouts may provide valid trading opportunities as well, but they fall beyond the scope of this strategy and so are overlooked.

One of the problems traders face is maintaining their focus, an issue that we discuss in much greater detail in a later chapter. What's more, just trading breakouts that originate from points of agreement generates approximately 100 trades per annum, which is more than enough opportunity for any trader.

Figure 11.2: breakout trading opportunity with trend lines

Source: MetaStock

Part mechanical, part eyeball search

Eyeballing each chart might sound a little onerous. If you prefer, you could use a mechanical search to help with the process. Note, however, that you will need to eyeball the results of the mechanical search to cover off the discretionary components of a valid breakout. I recommend you carry out a complete eyeball search about once a month as a back up and to hone your chart reading skills.

To do a mechanical search you need to formulate an exploration/ search in your own particular charting program using the breakout *quantitative* measures from chapter 10. I have tabulated these measures in table 11.1 for easy reference. You will find some codes for these in appendix B that are applicable to the charting program MetaStock. If you use a program other than MetaStock that has the ability to accept custom-built indicators, it shouldn't be too difficult to translate these formulae.

Table 11.1: quantitative measures required for a breakout pattern to be valid

Breakout candle — up	Breakout candle — down
Quantitative measures:	Quantitative measures:
• closes above the previous candle by more than half the ATR (17)	• closes below the previous candle by more than half the ATR (17)
• closes above its midpoint	• closes below its midpoint
• the MACD line is above its signal line and rising	• the MACD line is below its signal line and falling
• close is greater than 20 cents to help ensure there is sufficient liquidity.	• close is greater than $1 to help ensure there is room above zero for the price to continue falling for a reasonable period.

When the mechanical search has been done the resulting shares will need to be viewed and assessed for the *qualitative* measures required for a breakout pattern to be valid (see table 11.2).

Table 11.2: qualitative measures required for a breakout pattern to be valid

Breakout candle — up	Breakout candle — down
Qualitative measures:	Qualitative measures:
• breakout candle is preceded by a period of consolidation	• breakout candle is preceded by a period of consolidation
• it must close outside the triangle	• it must close outside the triangle
• the close is above the previous pivot point high.	• the close is below the previous pivot point low.

The example we have been looking at fits all of the criteria in the tables. I've highlighted only some of the criteria in figure 11.3 (it is simply impossible to highlight all of the criteria on a single chart).

Figure 11.3: example breakout with some of the breakout criteria highlighted

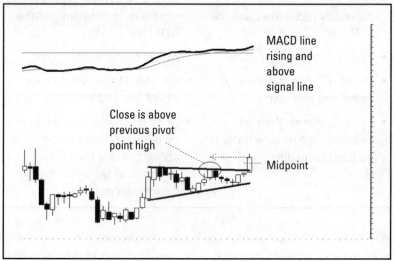

MACD line rising and above signal line

Close is above previous pivot point high

Midpoint

Source: MetaStock

Evaluating the breakouts

At this stage, we've searched our universe of shares for breakouts that should yield a shortlist of possibilities. If there is a need to reduce the shortlist further, I use the following extra characteristics (which were also discussed in chapter 10):

- there is strong volume with the breakout candle compared to the volume at the preceding POA

- there is a gap between the breakout candle and the preceding candle

- there is a Doji candle in or near the POA, prior to the breakout candle.

In the example trade, there is an increase in the volume with the breakout and there is also a Doji-like candle just prior to the breakout. I've highlighted these features in figure 11.4. These supporting characteristics will give us added confidence to commit to the trade.

When choosing a trade we also have to be mindful of sector risk. Guidelines for sector risk were given in chapter 4 and are certainly applicable to breakout trading, as they are also with active trading:

- maximum of 40 per cent of total capital per sector
- maximum of three positions per sector.

Figure 11.4: example breakout with some extra supporting characteristics

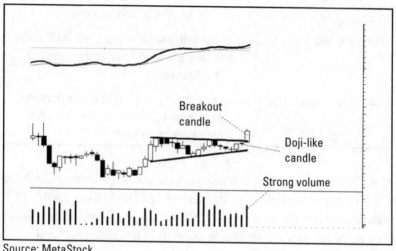

Source: MetaStock

Entry into a breakout trade

When a breakout opportunity has been selected we would normally enter the trade at the start of the following week. However, before we do enter at the beginning of the next week we need to calculate two things: how many shares to buy and the entry limit, so we don't chase the rally too far if the price jumps. Both of these calculations depend on the stop loss.

We therefore need to calculate the stop loss, then the entry limit and position size. Position sizing for breakout trading is done in exactly the same way as active investing and active trading, using the 2 per cent risk rule; that is, never risk more than 2 per cent of total capital in any individual trade (see chapter 4 for more about the 2 per cent rule). We must also observe the maximum position size limit of 20 per cent of total capital. This was also covered in chapter 4 under catastrophic risk management.

These calculations are summarised in table 11.3.

Table 11.3: summary of calculations before entering a trade

Calculate the stop loss:	There are two parts to the stop loss:
• initial stop loss	• initial stop loss is based on the theoretical POA
• trailing stop loss.	• trailing stop loss is 2 x the ATR (17) below the highest high of the trade for breaks to the upside.
Calculate the entry limit.	The entry limit is 2.5 x the ATR (17) above the stop loss at the point of the breakout.
Calculate the position size.	Use the 2 per cent risk rule and the stop loss to calculate the position size (see chapter 4).

In my *Breakout trading* newsletter all of these calculations are done for you for each new breakout trade identified by the strategy. Figure 11.5 is our example trade with the stop loss and the entry limit added. We're now ready to enter the market at the start of the following week.

Figure 11.5: breakout trade ready for entry

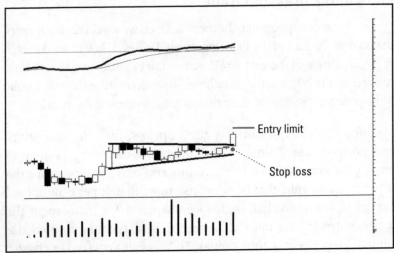

Source: MetaStock

When you come to place the trade it is important to ensure that you can get a price between the entry limit and the stop loss. You also need to ensure the share price hasn't jumped significantly since performing your calculations.

If we jump forward in time a few weeks (see figure 11.6) you can see where we would have entered the trade before the price moved above the entry limit. The week immediately after the breakout provided ample opportunity to enter the trade and it is quite common to have a week or two to enter the trade before the price moves beyond the entry limit. It is generally a good idea to act quickly when entering a breakout trade because the market will often take off very aggressively. Of course, this is exactly what we're hoping for.

Figure 11.6: example trade in progress

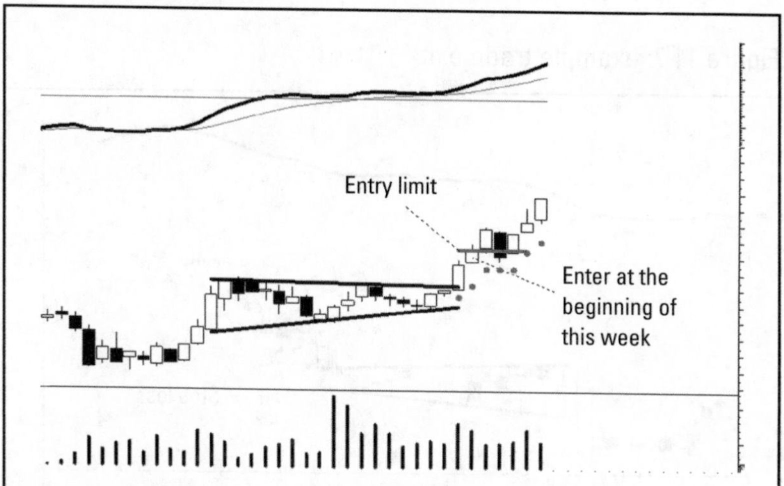

Source: MetaStock

Exit criteria

Finally, the only thing left to do is to monitor the trade and exit when a signal is given. Therefore, you need to call up the MACD indicator on your chart along with the price-related stop loss because either of these indicators could give the exit signal. For example, if the MACD line turns down during a breakout to the upside this would be an exit signal. On the other hand, if the price falls below the stop loss this will also trigger an exit.

This strategy is a weekly system and therefore acting on end-of-week signals is mandatory. However, there is the option to exit during the week if the price closes past the price-related stop loss at the end of the day. A trader may choose to do this if, for example, the market was in a very nervous and uncertain state. Daily stop loss execution is not necessarily better in terms of performance over weekly execution, but it does provide superior capital protection.

Figure 11.7 shows our example trade exit. You can see that the MACD line turned down, giving an exit signal. Note that in this particular trade the exit signal was given by the MACD momentum stop loss *before* the price-related stop loss was hit. Not all trades end this way, but it is nice when they do because it means we are getting out quickly, hopefully with plenty of profit in hand.

Figure 11.7: example trade exit

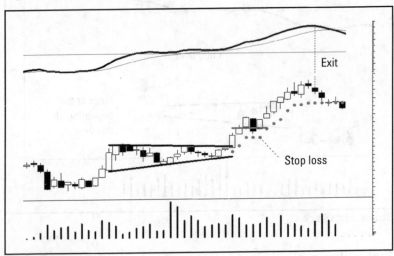

Source: MetaStock

The main components of the breakout trading plan are summarised below for easy reference. Overall, the breakout trading plan is a nimble, all-terrain trading system that is a great companion to the active trading strategy.

The main components of the breakout trading plan are as follows:

1 Search for valid breakouts.

2 Select a suitable trade from the valid breakouts:

    (a) Extra breakout characteristic guidelines

    (b) Sector risk guidelines

3 Calculate stop loss and entry limit.

4 Calculate position size (which mustn't exceed 20 per cent of total capital).

5 Enter the trade between the stop loss and the entry limit.

6 Exit if the MACD line turns *or* the price-related stop loss is triggered.

In chapter 12 Janice Korevaar trades the strategy for several weeks to give you a feel for how it operates in real time, using my weekly *Breakout trading* newsletter.

Chapter 12

Taking breakout trading for a test drive

This chapter is written by Janice Korevaar, who assists with the weekly production of the *Breakout trading* newsletter and with technical support for subscribers.

Now it's time to put the breakout trading strategy through its paces. This chapter will show you how Alan's strategy works in real time. You'll see how to enter a trade and when to exit.

During the six weeks of the simulation you will also witness one position closed out for a loss, and another for a profit, while the remainder of the trades continue on hold. All of this is part of the everyday trading process. By seeing each of the steps of this strategy executed in real time you will start to get a good feel for the rhythm of breakout trading.

This test run will be done in a similar manner to the test run for active trading in chapter 8. We will start with $100000 of trading capital and use the ActVest Trade Recorder to monitor the trades. For market information and ease of use, we will use the *Breakout trading* newsletter because it conveniently provides all the charts, signals and calculations we need to trade the breakout strategy.

Here is an outline of the steps we will be taking:

1 check open positions to see if there are any exits

2 check new trades to select a new trade if cash is available

3 work out details of the purchase; that is, position size

4 update records.

The simulation will start from the end of September 2010, which was when the *Breakout trading* newsletter was first launched, and will continue for six weeks. The charts that you will see in the simulation are taken directly from the *Breakout trading* newsletter and contain all the indicators that have been described to you in the last few chapters.

The charts in the newsletter also contain an extra indicator, the MACD bar, that is included to help subscribers read the direction of the MACD indicator on the charts more easily (see figure 12.1). It is colour coded in the newsletter. The direction of the MACD indicator is also listed in the newsletter data tables that we will use in this simulation.

Figure 12.1: example of a newsletter chart

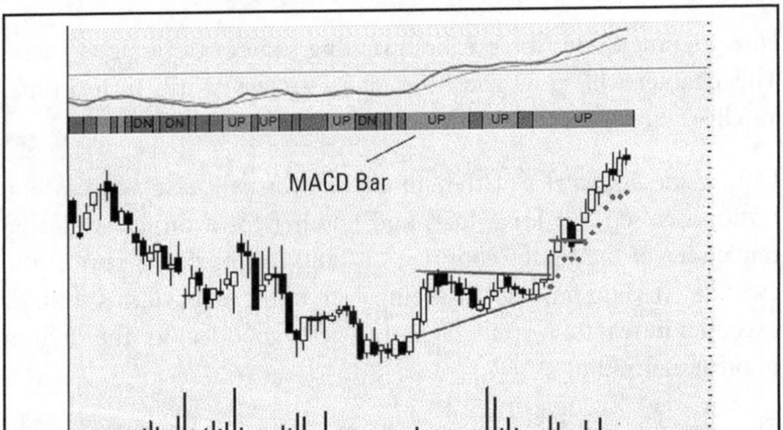

Source: MetaStock

Let's get started with $100 000 just prior to 24 September 2010. I've added $100 000 to the Trade Recorder in the cash on hand box (see figure 12.2).

Figure 12.2: trade recorder—start of the simulation

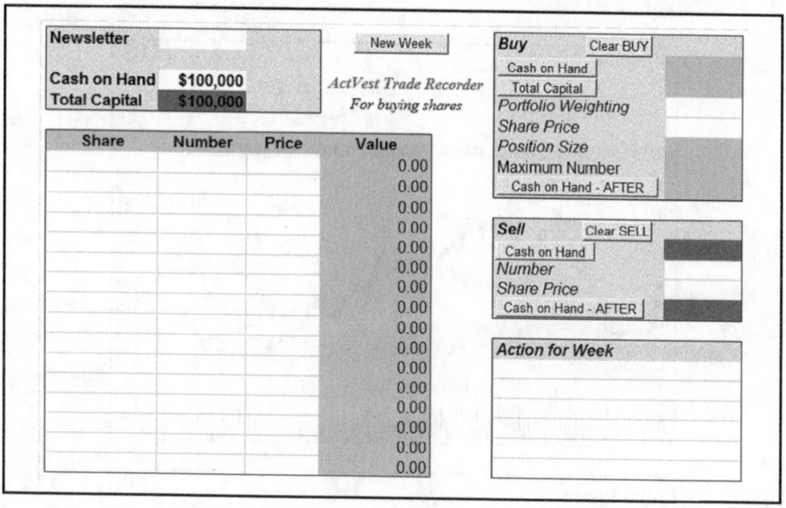

During this trading simulation, I employ a step-by-step checklist approach, starting with week 1.

Week 1—BTN100924, 24 September 2010

Routine	Commentary
Check open positions to see if there are any exits.	The new portfolio contains no current positions; therefore, there are no exits.
Check new trades to select a new trade if cash is available.	The following new trades are listed in this week's newsletter:
	AGS, ASX, API, HGG, WAN, WTP
	HGG is a break to the down side so we will not take this trade because we will not be short selling in this simulation. We will take all of the others (see figure 12.3, overleaf). There is no need to apply any extra analysis to these charts because we have the cash to purchase all that are available.

Figure 12.3: charts — new trades for BTN100924

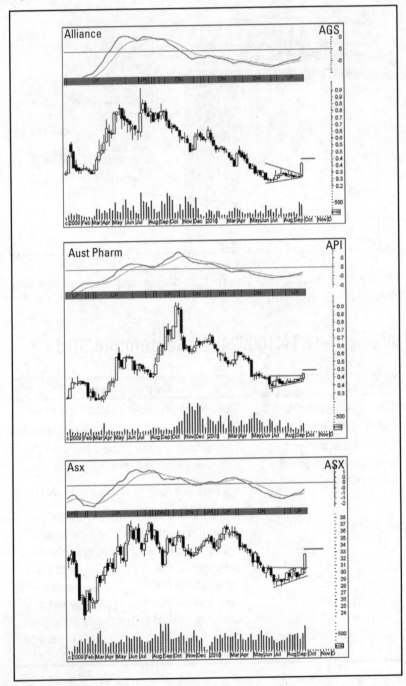

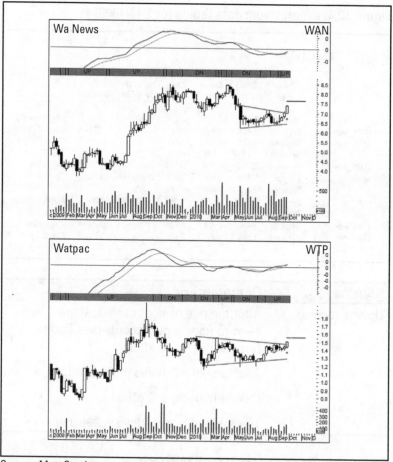

Source: MetaStock

Routine	Commentary
Work out details of the purchase; that is, position size.	The % Portfolio figures (for 2 per cent risk) in the data tables in figure 12.4 (overleaf) are used in the Trade Recorder to establish the position size for each share.

Figure 12.4: excerpt from data tables for BTN100924

Long Trades

Share Code	Trade Type	Closing Price($)	Entry Limit($)	Stop Loss($)	MACD Direction	%Portfolio	Action
ABC	Breakout	3.350	3.115	3.099	Up	20%	Check Entry
Buy ➡ AGS	Breakout	0.415	0.449	0.327	Up	7% ★	Check Entry
Buy ➡ API	Breakout	0.475	0.499	0.445	Up	20% ★	Check Entry
ASL	Breakout	2.180	2.058	1.876	Up	20%	Check Entry
Buy ➡ ASX	Breakout	32.710	33.420	30.002	Up	19% ★	Check Entry
BKN	Breakout	8.420	8.640	7.661	Up	17%	Check Entry
CAH	Breakout	2.020	1.879	1.970	Up		Hold
TRS	Breakout	17.350	18.216	16.500	Up	20%	Check Entry
TRY	Breakout	3.090	2.925	2.805	Up	20%	Check Entry
Buy ➡ WAN	Breakout	7.400	7.628	6.720	Up	17% ★	Check Entry
Buy ➡ WTP	Breakout	1.505	1.557	1.370	Up	17% ★	Check Entry

Routine	Commentary
Update records	After the purchase of our five shares we need to update our records (see Trade Recorder in figure 12.5).

The number of shares in the portfolio is five.

Cash remaining is $20 031.

The value of our portfolio is $99 999.

Figure 12.5: Trade Recorder for BTN100924

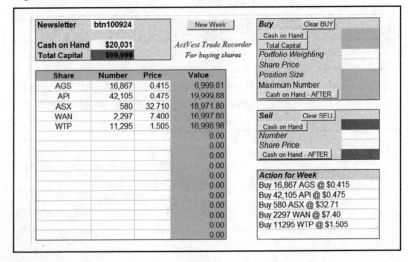

Week 2—BTN101001, 1 October 2010

Routine	Commentary
Check open positions to see if there are any exits.	The portfolio contains five current positions. In the data tables (see figure 12.6), AGS shows an exit signal due to the stop loss being hit (see figure 12.7, overleaf); therefore, we must sell AGS.

Figure 12.6: excerpt from data tables—BTN101001

	Share Code	Trade Type	Closing Price($)	Entry Limit($)	Stop Loss($)	MACD Direction	%Portfolio	Action
Long Trades								
	ABC	Breakout	3.480	3.115	3.193	Up		Hold
Sell ➡	AGS	Breakout	0.410	0.449	0.414	Up		Exit ★
	API	Breakout	0.520	0.499	0.465	Up	20%	Check Entry
	ASL	Breakout	2.160	2.058	1.941	Up	20%	Check Entry
	ASX	Breakout	32.280	33.420	31.265	Up	20%	Check Entry
	BKN	Breakout	8.390	8.640	7.842	Up	20%	Check Entry
	SUL	Breakout	6.450	6.252	5.925	Up	20%	Check Entry
Buy ➡	TPI	Breakout	1.195	1.256	1.090	Up	16% ★	Check Entry
	TRS	Breakout	17.770	18.216	16.500	Up	20%	Check Entry
	TRY	Breakout	3.340	2.925	2.962	Up		Hold
	WAN	Breakout	7.170	7.628	6.746	Up	20%	Check Entry
Buy ➡	WDS	Breakout	0.540	0.632	0.438	Up	7% ★	Check Entry
	WTP	Breakout	1.530	1.557	1.412	Up	20%	Check Entry

Figure 12.7: exit signal for AGS — BTN101001

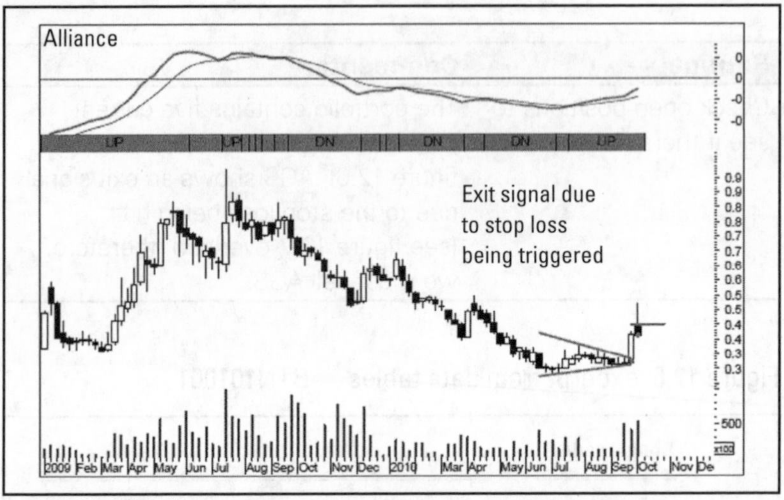

Source: MetaStock

Routine	Commentary
Check new trades to select a new trade if cash is available.	After the sale of AGS, there is about $26000 cash available, which will probably enable us to buy two new positions this week. The following new trades are listed in this week's newsletter (the charts are shown in figure 12.8): GXY, TPI, WDS The extra guidelines for assessing breakout candles from chapter 10 were used to select TPI and WDS, which both show an increase in volume with the breakout, where GXY did not. Therefore, we will buy TPI & WDS.

Figure 12.8: charts — new trades, BTN101001

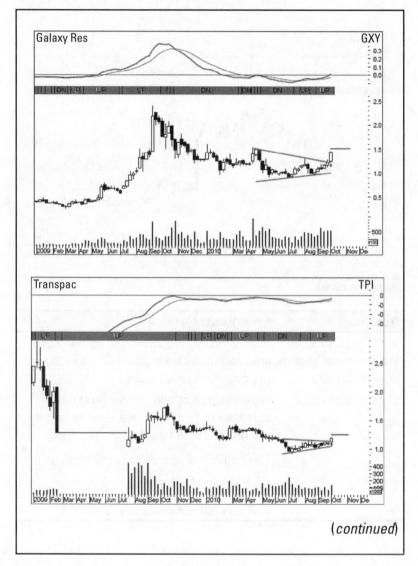

(*continued*)

Figure 12.8 (*cont'd*): charts—new trades, BTN101001

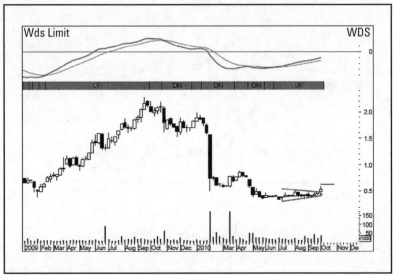

Source: MetaStock

Routine	Commentary
Work out details of the purchase; that is, position size.	The % Portfolio figures in the data tables are used in the Trade Recorder to establish the position in each share.
Update records	After the sale of one position and the purchase of two more, we need to update our records (see figure 12.9).
	The number of shares in our portfolio is six.
	Cash remaining is $3644.
	The value of our portfolio is $101 314.

Figure 12.9: Trade Recorder—BTN101001

Newsletter	btn101001		
Cash on Hand	$3,644		
Total Capital	$101,314		

New Week

ActVest Trade Recorder
For buying shares

Share	Number	Price	Value
API	42,105	0.520	21,894.60
ASX	580	32.280	18,722.40
TPI	13,565	1.195	16,210.18
WAN	2,297	7.170	16,469.49
WDS	13,133	0.540	7,091.82
WTP	11,295	1.530	17,281.35
			0.00
			0.00
			0.00
			0.00
			0.00
			0.00
			0.00
			0.00
			0.00

Buy   Clear BUY

Cash on Hand
Total Capital
Portfolio Weighting
Share Price
Position Size
Maximum Number
Cash on Hand - AFTER

Sell   Clear SELL

Cash on Hand
Number
Share Price
Cash on Hand - AFTER

Action for Week
Sell 16,867 AGS @ $0.41
Buy 13,565 TPI @ $1.195
Buy 13,133 WDS @ $0.54

Week 3—BTN101008, 8 October 2010

Routine	Commentary
Check open positions to see if there are any exits.	The portfolio contains six current positions. In the data tables (see figure 12.10, overleaf) there are no exit signals for our shares, so no selling is required this week.
Check new trades to select a new trade if cash is available.	There is not enough cash for any new position, so no buying is required this week.
Work out details of the purchase; that is, position size	No buying required this week
Update records	There was no selling or buying this week but we can, if we wish, update our records with the current value of our positions (see figure 12.11, overleaf).
	The number of shares in our portfolio is six.
	Cash remaining is $3644.
	The value of our portfolio is $105 329.

Figure 12.10: excerpt from data table — BTN101008

Long Trades

Share Code	Trade Type	Closing Price($)	Entry Limit($)	Stop Loss($)	MACD Direction	%Portfolio	Action
ABC	Breakout	3.520	3.115	3.226	Up		Hold
AGO	Breakout	2.550	2.671	2.220	Up	12%	Check Entry
API	Breakout	0.545	0.499	0.465	Up	20%	Check Entry
ASL	Breakout	2.220	2.058	1.941	Up	20%	Check Entry
ASX	Breakout	33.800	33.420	31.377	Up	20%	Check Entry
BKN	Breakout	8.320	8.640	7.842	Up	20%	Check Entry
SUL	Breakout	6.750	6.252	6.066	Up	20%	Check Entry
TPI	Breakout	1.255	1.256	1.090	Up	14%	Check Entry
TRS	Breakout	18.040	18.216	16.704	Up	20%	Check Entry
TRY	Breakout	3.490	2.925	3.075	Up		Hold
WAN	Breakout	7.140	7.628	6.746	Up	20%	Check Entry
WDS	Breakout	0.560	0.632	0.451	Up	7%	Check Entry
WTP	Breakout	1.625	1.557	1.451	Up	20%	Check Entry

Figure 12.11: Trade Recorder — BTN101008

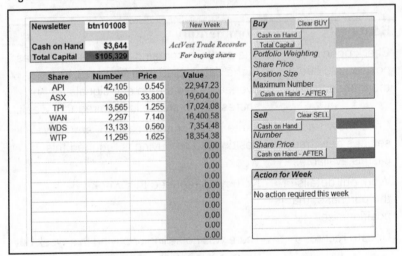

Week 4—BTN101015, 15 October 2010

Routine	Commentary
Check open positions to see if there are any exits.	The portfolio contains six current positions. In the data tables (see figure 12.12) there are no exit signals for our shares, so no selling is required this week.
Check new trades to select a new trade if cash is available.	There is not enough cash for any new position, so no buying is required this week.
Work out details of the purchase; that is, position size.	No buying is required this week.
Update records	There was no selling or buying this week but we can, if we wish, update our records with the current value of our positions (see figure 12.13, overleaf).

The number of shares in our portfolio is six.

Cash remaining is $3644.

The value of our portfolio is $105 803. |

Figure 12.12: excerpt from data tables—BTN101015

Long Trades							
Share Code	Trade Type	Closing Price($)	Entry Limit($)	Stop Loss($)	MACD Direction	%Portfolio	Action
ABC	Breakout	3.520	3.115	3.226	Up		Hold
AGO	Breakout	2.680	2.671	2.293	Up	13%	Check Entry
API	Breakout	0.520	0.499	0.485	Up	20%	Check Entry
ASL	Breakout	2.220	2.058	2.002	Up	20%	Check Entry
ASX	Breakout	33.750	33.420	31.689	Up	20%	Check Entry
BKN	Breakout	8.200	8.640	7.842	Down		Exit
SUL	Breakout	6.650	6.252	6.087	Up	20%	Check Entry
TPI	Breakout	1.320	1.256	1.133	Up	18%	Check Entry
TRS	Breakout	18.180	18.216	16.902	Up	20%	Check Entry
TRY	Breakout	3.520	2.925	3.179	Up		Hold
WAN	Breakout	7.180	7.628	6.746	Up	20%	Check Entry
WDS	Breakout	0.600	0.632	0.451	Up	7%	Check Entry
WTP	Breakout	1.630	1.557	1.506	Up	20%	Check Entry

Figure 12.13: Trade Recorder—BTN101015

Newsletter	btn101015				New Week			Buy		Clear BUY
					ActVest Trade Recorder			Cash on Hand		
Cash on Hand	$3,644				*For buying shares*			Total Capital		
Total Capital	$105,803							Portfolio Weighting		
								Share Price		
Share	Number	Price	Value					Position Size		
API	42,105	0.520	21,894.60					Maximum Number		
ASX	580	33.750	19,575.00					Cash on Hand - AFTER		
TPI	13,565	1.320	17,905.80							
WAN	2,297	7.180	16,492.46					Sell		Clear SELL
WDS	13,133	0.600	7,879.80					Cash on Hand		
WTP	11,295	1.630	18,410.85					Number		
			0.00					Share Price		
			0.00					Cash on Hand - AFTER		
			0.00							
			0.00					Action for Week		
			0.00							
			0.00					No action required this week		
			0.00							
			0.00							
			0.00							
			0.00							

Week 5—BTN101022, 22 October 2010

Routine	Commentary
Check open positions to see if there are any exits.	The portfolio contains six current positions. In the data tables (see figure 12.14) there are no exit signals for our shares, so no selling is required this week.
Check new trades to select a new trade if cash is available.	There is not enough cash for any new position, so no buying is required this week.
Work out details of the purchase; that is, position size.	No buying is required this week.
Update records	There was no selling or buying this week but we can, if we wish, update our records with the current value of our positions (see figure 12.15). The number of shares in our portfolio is six. Cash remaining is $3644. The value of our portfolio is $105 765.

Figure 12.14: excerpt from data tables — BTN101022

Long Trades

Share Code	Trade Type	Closing Price($)	Entry Limit($)	Stop Loss($)	MACD Direction	%Portfolio	Action
ABC	Breakout	3.600	3.115	3.282	Up		Hold
AGO	Breakout	2.540	2.671	2.293	Up	15%	Check Entry
API	Breakout	0.495	0.499	0.485	Up	20%	Check Entry
ASL	Breakout	2.380	2.058	2.093	Up		Hold
ASX	Breakout	34.960	33.420	32.137	Up	20%	Check Entry
BLY	Breakout	3.770	3.851	3.292	Up	13%	Check Entry
SUL	Breakout	6.600	6.252	6.087	Up	20%	Check Entry
TPI	Breakout	1.270	1.256	1.203	Up	20%	Check Entry
TRS	Breakout	18.020	18.216	16.902	Up	20%	Check Entry
TRY	Breakout	3.290	2.925	3.179	Up		Hold
WAN	Breakout	7.280	7.628	6.746	Up	19%	Check Entry
WDS	Breakout	0.615	0.632	0.451	Up	6%	Check Entry
WTP	Breakout	1.680	1.557	1.518	Up	20%	Check Entry

Figure 12.15: Trade Recorder — BTN101022

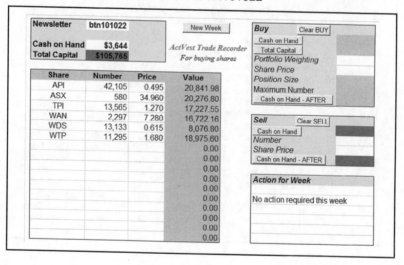

Week 6—BTN101029, 29 October 2010

Routine	Commentary
Check open positions to see if there are any exits.	The portfolio contains six current positions. In the data tables (see figure 12.16) ASX has an exit signal due to the stop loss being triggered, so we must sell ASX (as it happens, for a profit). The chart of ASX is shown in figure 12.17.

Figure 12.16: excerpt from data tables—BTN101029

Long Trades

	Share Code	Trade Type	Closing Price($)	Entry Limit($)	Stop Loss($)	MACD Direction	%Portfolio	Action
	ABC	Breakout	3.580	3.115	3.294	Up		Hold
	AGO	Breakout	2.510	2.671	2.293	Up	16%	Check Entry
	AJL	Breakout	2.390	2.625	1.999	Up	9%	Check Entry
	ANZ	Breakout	24.810	25.594	23.850	Up	20%	Check Entry
	API	Breakout	0.515	0.499	0.485	Up	20%	Check Entry
	ASL	Breakout	2.390	2.058	2.119	Up		Hold
Exit ➡	ASX	Breakout	37.100	33.420	40.051	Up		Exit ★
	BLY	Breakout	3.620	3.851	3.292	Up	15%	Check Entry
	SUL	Breakout	6.670	6.252	6.109	Up	20%	Check Entry
	TPI	Breakout	1.230	1.256	1.203	Up	20%	Check Entry
	TRS	Breakout	18.400	18.216	17.330	Up	20%	Check Entry
	TRY	Breakout	3.350	2.925	3.179	Up		Hold
	WAN	Breakout	7.160	7.628	6.746	Up	20%	Check Entry
	WDS	Breakout	0.680	0.632	0.515	Up	10%	Check Entry
	WHC	Breakout	6.960	7.235	6.350	Up	17%	Check Entry
	WTP	Breakout	1.665	1.557	1.518	Up	20%	Check Entry

Figure 12.17: exit signal for ASX—BTN101029

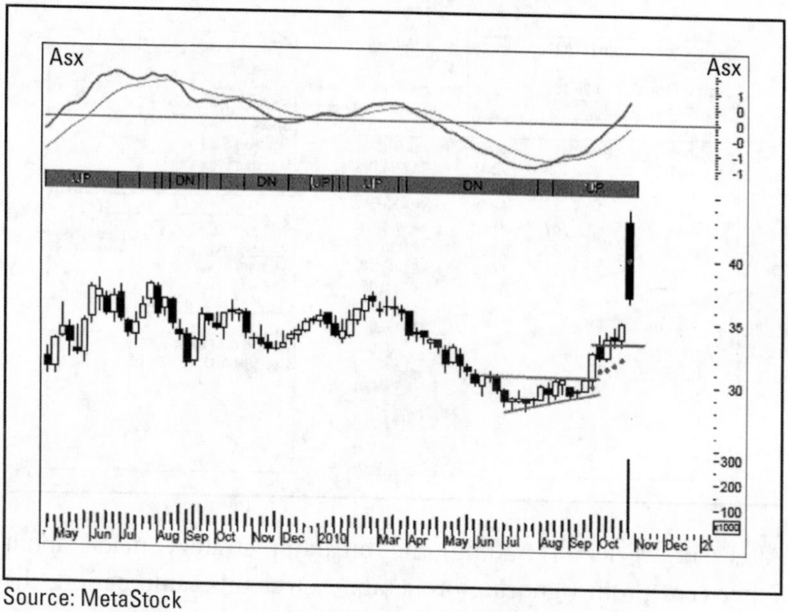

Source: MetaStock

Routine	Commentary
Check new trades to select a new trade if cash is available.	There is cash available from the sale of ASX for another new position. However, this is the end of the simulation so no purchase will be made.
Work out details of the purchase; that is, position size.	No buying is required this week.
Update records	We have updated our records (see figure 12.18, overleaf).
	The number of shares in our portfolio is five.
	Cash remaining is $25 162.
	The value of our portfolio is $107 714.

Figure 12.18: Trade Recorder—BTN101029

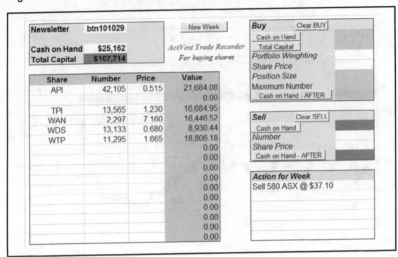

After six weeks of trading, the breakout strategy made about 7 per cent profit (ignoring brokerage). Over this same period, the All Ordinaries index moved a little over 1 per cent.

Apart from witnessing the strategy generating a profit, I hope that you were able to see how easy it is to drive the system and appreciate the value in having a routine to follow.

Breakout trading is a valuable addition to every trader's tool box. It is a versatile, nimble strategy that can provide trading opportunities even when the market is going sideways. The *Breakout trading* newsletter provides subscribers with all the information they need to trade the strategy and you will find a subscription form located near the back of this book. As with the *ActTrade* newsletter, if you subscribe with this form you will receive a complimentary copy of the ActVest Trade Recorder, normally valued at $49.50. Furthermore, if you would like a sample of a recent copy of the *Breakout trading* newsletter, send an email request to enquiries@alanhull.com.

In part IV, you're in for something completely different as Alan discusses matters that are less technical than trading simulations.

PART IV

In conclusion

Chapter 13

The biggest problem is you

If I had followed much of the commonsense advice that was given to me when I started share trading I would have enjoyed a lot more trading success than I have. The reason I didn't is simple: I either sabotaged myself through a lack of emotional discipline, or I stubbornly pursued fanciful trading strategies that appealed to my intellect, but provided little sustenance to my bank account.

I've been for the obligatory ride on the psychological rollercoaster like all other seasoned share traders and I don't think there's any way of avoiding it. The only share traders I've talked to who haven't been through a similar experience are the ones who quit share trading before they got that far.

In part IV we look at some of the more peripheral aspects of share trading, but don't underestimate their importance to your trading success. Probably the most important of all is trading psychology. In fact, I would go so far as to say that the biggest obstacle between you and trading success is you.

The idea of share trading

Wannabe share traders are typically aged from 25 to 40—they are keen to escape the rat race as fast as they can and are usually willing to part with large amounts of money in order to do so. Sadly, they often fall victim to unscrupulous 'get rich quick' product vendors who promise very simple-to-drive, off-the-shelf trading solutions that have very large price tags—payable upfront, of course.

Quite a few readers won't have managed to get this far into the book because they've already lost interest and decided share trading is not for them; at least, not the way it's prescribed by me, anyway. If that is the case, buying this book was probably money well spent because now they're free to pursue other ways to make money—ways that they will enjoy and therefore will have a much better chance of succeeding at.

But for those who choose to stick it out, here are some of the hurdles you're going to have to jump over at some point:

- greed
- fear
- confidence
- procrastination
- ego
- frustration
- anger
- laziness
- stubbornness.

I could tackle each of these key aspects of trading psychology, one by one, in a fairly clinical manner. But I believe it's probably best if I just elaborate on some of my own experiences, along with some of the knowledge and observations I've accumulated over the years from teaching other people to trade.

Show me the money

I'll start by going back to a time when I was more in love with the proceeds from share trading than I was with the actual process of share trading; in other words, a time when I was in love with the lure of the almighty dollar. This is no doubt one of the more common pitfalls for share traders who, if they're anything like me, become more focused on the money they're making than the shares they're trading.

Trading the stock market is all about understanding its behaviour and exploiting that behaviour for profit. But the stock market is in a constant state of flux and if you take your eye off the ball, it will very quickly slip away from you. Greed is seductive and will work hard to distract you. Greed usually appears when you've had some success and your bank balance has begun to swell.

Another way to explain this problem is with a simple analogy: imagine if the surgeons operating on you were thinking about their fee rather than focusing on the operation they were performing. I don't particularly fancy people standing over me with a scalpel while their minds are doing sums, trying to figure out whether or not they can afford to fly business class to Tahiti for their holidays.

They wouldn't be much of a surgeon and you won't be much of a share trader if you function the same way. I know, because I've tried it. The flip side to greed is fear, which can also have us focusing on the money rather than our share trading.

Do you have the stomach for it?

Share trading is all about having the balance of probability working in our favour. To succeed over the long term we only have to tip the scale of probability ever so slightly in our direction. But while most of us have a clear understanding of the science of probability, not all of us have the stomach for it.

To illustrate my point, let's go back to the simple game of coin toss from chapter 4, where the payouts are even, making it a fair game of chance. Everyone agrees that when tossing a coin, the probable outcome is evenly split between heads and tails, a 50:50 proposition.

While the probable outcome of tossing a coin is an even split between heads and tails, it doesn't mean that the outcome will oscillate perfectly between heads and tails in a flip/flop head, tail, head, tail, head, tail pattern. It does mean that the balance of outcomes will always return to the centre line of zero at some point. Based on my exercise of 100 coin tosses in figure 4.1 on p. 51 (which is in no way conclusive and is for illustrative purposes only), however, it appears it can deviate by as much as seven and it is this deviation that can be hard to stomach.

Assume you're betting on tails in our game of coin toss and you're down by five tosses after the 21st game. In other words, you have lost 13 games and won only eight. At this point, most people will want to inspect the coin and maybe have a turn at tossing it.

Miraculously the odds swing in your favour and you find that you're ahead by seven tosses at the end of the thirty-ninth game. Your opponent is now beginning to question the fairness of the game.

Now let's assume you don't get to witness the game of coin toss. Both players are simply being given the results of the game, played at another location, by a supposedly reliable third party, such as the Australian Securities Exchange. If you were down 13 losses to eight wins, would you drop out of the game because you believed there was a bias in the process—especially if the wager on each game is $1000?

Unfortunately, this is a common occurrence in the stock market, particularly during tough times. Instead of maintaining faith in our strategy when we suffer a losing streak, we become preoccupied with our mounting losses and simply bail out of the market.

Sadly, many novice traders will prove a strategy through comprehensive backtesting, only to dismiss it as a failure after trading it in real time for as little as 10 trades. It appears they just don't have the stomach for probability. Their ability to maintain their objectivity is lost because their back pocket nerves eventually override all other thinking by transmitting ever-increasing pain signals to the brain.

To preserve your trading capital in the face of mounting losses, I recommend sticking to the 2 per cent risk rule. To overcome your fear in the face of mounting losses, I recommend carrying a coin. You never know when you might have to play a game of coin toss and prove to yourself that a string of up to 10 (or even more) consecutive losses is very possible.

We tend to project our current circumstances onto the future. When we're suffering a losing streak, we believe that this is the way it's going to be forever. What's more, this manner of thinking applies equally to both men and women but, interestingly, there are some key aspects of trading psychology that appear to be gender specific.

Men love to hunt

In chapter 5 we broke the process of trading into several key components (or tasks) and one of these was to search for trading opportunities. I just love to hunt down those winning shares! What's more, I'm not alone, because many other male share traders appear to have the same passion.

On the other hand it is somewhat disheartening when I'm running a workshop on risk management at a trading and investing expo and hardly anyone turns up. Usually they're all next door (the men, anyway) in a seminar titled 'Learn how to spot hot stocks' or something similar, learning how to capture those winning shares. There's no doubt that men are the hunter/gatherers and this applies to fishing, shooting, bargain hunting on eBay and share trading.

There's a bit of a downside to this because men are somewhat reluctant to part with those beloved shares they've worked so hard to track down. We tend to get emotionally attached to our hot stocks and therefore we're inclined to ignore our stop losses when it's time to sell.

This is where the female share trader comes to the fore because they're far more passionate about protecting their trading capital than any silly shares that their male counterparts may have taken a fancy to. Female traders are typically far better at executing their stop losses than men and so, where possible, trading as a team with your spouse is generally a good idea.

You're only as sick as your secrets

There's another advantage to trading with your spouse—you probably won't be able to keep any secrets. This is a good thing because one of the best pieces of advice I've ever been given is 'You're only as sick as your secrets'. This applies to life in general, but definitely to share trading as well.

On the subject of greed, I got so focused on the money I was making and the fancy new car I was going to buy that I completely took my eyes off the market. When you're trading derivatives this is definitely not a good thing. A friend brought the market back into focus for me when he asked how I was coping with the sudden downturn in the markets over the past few days. I immediately jumped on my computer and discovered, to my horror, that I'd lost $34 000 in just two days.

I was devastated by this loss. I immediately withdrew from the market and spent several weeks psychologically and financially regrouping. This was simply a case of a lapse in trading discipline brought about by success.

It's a fact of life that the pain we endure is what makes us grow. We enjoy the good times, but learn life's lessons when things go wrong. This is on one proviso — that we take responsibility for our decisions and actions and not try to make excuses or pretend they didn't happen. This is why many stock market participants use brokers — they have someone to blame when things go wrong. You can't make these excuses when you're a self-directed share trader.

Network with other traders

I strongly recommend trading with a buddy, whether it's your spouse or someone else, so you can keep each other honest and learn from your mistakes. Trading clubs are also available in most capital cities in Australia and even in many major country towns. If there isn't one near you, maybe you can start one like I did.

I convene the Sunday Traders Club (STC) in Melbourne, which meets six times a year (there's an STC in Sydney and Brisbane as well). These clubs are run on a non-profit basis. If you would like to know more about them, send me an email enquiry via my website at <www.alanhull.com>. I can put you on my email database and you'll receive notifications of club meetings and related events.

Share trading is a very isolating activity and I can't stress enough the importance of networking with other traders. Like the loneliness of the long distance runner, share traders spend a lot of time by themselves and this can be dangerous. We tend to amplify our own thoughts by playing them repeatedly over and over in our heads, convincing ourselves that we're right, and this inevitably leads to a loss of perspective.

However, discussing our thoughts with others who can provide us with an objective and unemotional point of view is often of great benefit. I see my friend Mark, to whom I have dedicated this book, once or twice a week, when we talk about what's going on in our lives and bounce ideas off each other. We have no personal stake in each other's businesses, so we can provide an unbiased and objective point of view.

Experience will numb you

Of course, time in the market and experiencing losses repeatedly over many years of trading will ultimately numb you to their emotional impact. The psychological rollercoaster that you experience in the early days will inevitably start to level out at some point. The trick is to last the distance, so here's a little tip—learn to say 'whoops' a lot.

I say it to myself whenever a trade goes wrong and I lose money. I say 'whoops', close out the trade and move on. It helps to desensitise me to the losses and, given how long I've been saying it to myself, has become a subconscious signal for me to keep moving forward.

Recruits being trained to trade on a trading floor in a manual exchange (which are largely a thing of the past) used to start off by simply trading: buy and sell, buy and sell. The idea was that the recruits wouldn't worry about making or losing money, but just practice pulling the trigger. When the new floor trader learns to pull the trigger without any hesitation, they start to work on making money.

Here the message is the same: you need to learn how to lose money as much as you need to learn how to make money, so you won't be afraid of suffering losses and you won't freeze when you need to act. So whenever you lose money, say 'whoops'. After 10 years or more, you'll be as good at losing money as I am.

Easy does it, but do it

But here's the catch: you won't get market experience and become numb to your losses until you get in there and start trading in earnest. There is no holy grail solution that will make you bulletproof and immune to losses, so don't waste your time looking for it. We become share traders through experience, much the same as a carpenter becomes competent by getting on a building site and swinging a hammer. Attending trade school will only get you so far.

You need to start share trading if you want to grow as a trader and learn your weaknesses. That's when the reality of trading starts and the self-understanding begins. I often say to novice traders that the stock market teaches them how to trade and all I'm going to do is show them how to survive long enough to learn the lessons.

I haven't really done the topic of trading psychology justice in this one short chapter and therefore I strongly recommend that you make the effort to seek out other books that specialise in this area. I found that after I'd been trading for a while, I would go back and re-read the same books on psychology, and they would take on a whole new meaning and level of importance.

I do know that you've got to want to be a share trader badly enough to cop the pain that you will inevitably have to endure. That pain will be both financial and psychological. At some point you will stand at the crossroads and ask yourself the question, 'how badly do I want to be a trader?' The rewards are there to be had, but share trading isn't for everyone and there is a price of admission—other than money.

Chapter 14

Keep your eye on the ball

In this chapter, we talk about maintaining our focus. I've got some bad news: the noise in the marketplace is deafening and it's only going to get louder as time goes on. This is where technology is working against us rather than for us, by bombarding us with information through a vast array of different communication media, including newspapers, magazines, radio, television, the internet and even our mobile phones. Combine all these communication portals with the different information, product and service providers, and the permutations are virtually endless. It's no wonder I'm often approached by novice traders who are more confused about share trading after several months of initial investigation than they were at the outset.

Swimming with sharks

We need to access certain information vendors and service providers, but we have to block out the vast majority of market noise. As you'll soon discover, you're swimming with sharks in the marketplace and all those service providers out there who want so badly to be your friend are more often than not simply trying to advance their own agenda, rather than assist you with yours.

So your job, firstly, is to know your own agenda and, secondly, to be aware of their agenda. You either then make use of their services or block them out. When you've completed this process you definitely have to focus on share trading and not allow yourself to be sidetracked. I'm going to look at a few of the more common distractions that traders face and hopefully this will help you to deal with and/or reject them.

Product providers, whoever they are and whatever they do, will prey on our psychology. In the case of financial service providers, it's usually our sense of greed and fear that they are likely to try to tap into. We are also tempted by activities that appear exciting and glamorous, and this is another foible that marketeers exploit.

A sense of excitement

A classic example is where the media has managed to take a lot of fairly dull financial market information and make it sound as exciting as a day at the races. If you're ever awake late at night and you have access to pay TV, tune in to the overseas business channel (usually CNN or similar) and listen to the open of the US stock markets. Close your eyes and listen rather than watch because the commentary is often something akin to someone calling a horse race, with its upbeat tempo and dramatic phrasing:

> That's the opening bell and we've got eyes on both the NYSE and the NASDAQ to see which market's going to take the early initiative. I can see that Microsoft is still reeling from the SEC's unfavourable ruling and that will no doubt have a greater impact on the tech heavy NASDAQ than the NYSE. But it looks like General Electric is also going to be a drag on the NYSE with its overnight disclosure of increased tax liabilities. So let's take a look at the early numbers...

This sense of excitement is further enhanced by the strong promotion of intraday trading in the US by product vendors who provide up-to-the-second information via the internet.

The reality is that share trading is a relatively dull and boring process that involves a great deal of repetition. This is also the case with intraday trading, where the trading tactics need to be very simplistic in order to facilitate very fast decision making.

The Australian business channels are definitely more subtle than their US counterparts, but there's no question that the local media is also making a concerted effort to make financial news seem far more exciting and dramatic than it really is.

The narrative fallacy

Another tactic that the media employs is the use of narration in communicating, which can be a distortion of the facts.

We all love a good story and story telling has always been a craft that attracts an audience. No-one is more adept at story telling than the media, which has turned it into an art form through decades of practice. Let me illustrate how the media does this, starting with a simple set of facts:

- oil prices continue to rise
- the US Federal Reserve is due to meet later this week
- global financial markets have fallen for the past two days.

These facts are then packaged together into a single narrative that is far more digestible:

> Global financial markets continue to weaken on concerns that the US Fed will try to head off the threat of inflation due to rising oil prices, when it meets in a couple of days' time.

This narrative is someone's interpretation of the facts and is potentially highly misleading. The media is highly skilled at making opinion and conjecture sound like facts, so it is therefore imperative that if you're going to follow financial news you learn to separate facts from conjecture.

Let's take a step back for a moment and look at why we have a preference for the narrative over the simple set of facts. The best way to demonstrate is with an example that uses numbers. Firstly, I'll ask you to study the following seven numbers for approximately five seconds and try to remember them:

3   5   7   9   11   13   15

Now try to remember the following seven numbers:

13   2   21   17   5   1   14

In the first instance it's relatively easy to remember the numbers because you can quickly detect a pattern and therefore compress the information that you have to retain. However, in the second instance there's no shortcut and you simply have to remember seven different numbers, which is clearly a good deal harder. Our brains love to conserve memory space and energy, and using pattern recognition helps us to do this. We therefore have a desire to fit a story or narrative to a set of unrelated data, a phenomenon known as the narrative fallacy.

Now that you're aware of the narrative fallacy, you'll hopefully be on your guard, so when you hear the newsreader declare that 'The stock market fell today because …', you'll know it's a mixture of fact and speculation.

Sometimes we just don't know

No-one in the media wants to say 'I don't know'. Imagine the newsreader saying, 'the market rose today and we have no idea why'. But sometimes we just don't know why the market behaved the way it did.

In the short term in particular, much of the market's behaviour is effectively random because it is the net outcome of millions of individual variables that we can't possibly hope to measure and/or assimilate. Most of the time, the market goes up or down and there is no single, discrete cause. The media makes the market's behaviour seem logical and deterministic, but share traders have to operate in real time and making simplistic conjectures with the benefit of hindsight is a luxury we don't have.

Don't think you're stupid because a newsreader makes the market sound very straightforward. No-one in the newsroom knows what's going to happen in the markets tomorrow anymore than you do. In fact, I've seen market analysis in the media get it completely wrong on many occasions—even with the benefit of hindsight!

There is one other way of dealing with the financial news media and that is to not listen to it unless you have to. This approach works well for anyone who is a self-directed share trader, like me, because we don't need to have regular access to financial news.

Unlike the media, however, dealing with stock brokers is unavoidable for anyone who wants to buy and sell shares.

Stockbrokers

Dealing with stockbrokers can be a very rewarding experience, but they can also lead you well and truly up the garden path. Let's look at two kinds of stockbroker—full service and online.

A full service broker is not paid to give advice, but they provide this service so that you will pay a premium to have them execute your trades. The advice is a value add.

They can also provide access to products and services not normally available through an online broking service, such as access to an initial public offering (IPO) or specific company research that isn't readily available elsewhere. Full service brokers can also execute your trades while you're busy doing something else, freeing you from having to sit in front of a computer screen and do it all yourself.

If you're paying a full service broker a premium to execute your trades, make sure that there's a good reason. The difference in price between a full service broker and an online broking service is considerable and while I'm in no way against using full service brokers, you should have a good reason for using them. I use a full service broker and an online broking service. In a similar vein, you also need to be clear on what market(s) you are trading and what products you're dealing in.

Don't be seduced

This book is about share trading, not currency trading, index trading, bond trading or commodity trading. I'm not an 'everything' trader, but a lot of product vendors make it sound like being an 'everything' trader is as easy as falling out of bed. They boast how their online trading platforms can give you up-to-the-microsecond information on just about any financial market anywhere in the world and how you can trade just about any financial instrument with a simple touch of a button.

There's only one catch: it's taken me most of my life to learn how to trade the Australian sharemarket successfully, so how could I possibly hope to competently trade other financial instruments in offshore markets that I know little to nothing about? The bottom line is that these product vendors aren't overly concerned about the financial wellbeing of their individual customers, but are simply trying to market their global trading platforms as far and as widely as possible.

They love catchy phrases such as 'global access', 'with just the touch of a button', 'all from the comfort of your living room' and even 'stop making someone else rich'. It's all about getting as many people locked into their service as they can and in many cases their marketing approach sounds more suited to promoting a casino than a broking service. Take foreign exchange (FX) trading, for instance. The key features that many online FX brokers tout are:

- global FX markets are open 24 hours a day
- access leverage up to 100 times your trading capital
- trade worldwide from Asia to the US, and even Europe!

If I were a gambler, these attributes would be very appealing—but I'm not a gambler. What's more, trading foreign exchange, which is the interface between two different currency markets, is one of the hardest forms of trading I know of. The idea that 'Banks make their money this way and so can you' is laughable because the banks are using scale of economy that, as small private traders, we simply don't have access to.

I know I'm probably bursting a few bubbles, but the broking industry, thanks largely to the online revolution, has become a discounting machine that employs many forms of seductive marketing. It is imperative that as a trader I stick to what I know and choose a broking service that will facilitate my needs, not seduce me into trading markets and financial products that I know nothing about. There is no shorter path to ruin!

Trading programs

Another group of product promoters in the seduction business are the trading program vendors who sell very overpriced trading software that will tell you what to buy and when to buy and sell it. These vendors aren't to be confused with legitimate software providers such as Equis, the creators of MetaStock, or other sellers of legitimate charting programs. Virtually all legitimate charting programs cost less than $2000. Dubious promoters of trading programs are usually easily spotted because their products sell for ridiculous amounts of money, such as $5000 or more. The annual subscription fee is also well into the thousands, where most legitimate data services cost less than $1000 per year.

These get-rich-quick products are easily spotted, but they appeal to many would-be share traders who simply don't want to put in the hard work that's required to be a self-directed share trader (we discussed this in chapter 1). They're prepared to part with a large amount of money and take the gamble that they may have just found the shortcut they've been hoping for that will take them to the promised land with very little effort.

One other common hallmark of these 'black box' trading solutions is that they often originate from overseas and are sold locally by an 'authorised' Australian agent. This agency arrangement is needed to overcome our fairly strict licensing regime that's designed to keep Australian consumers safe. Of course, when things go horribly wrong, the overseas product provider blames the agent and the agent blames the overseas product provider. In the meantime the consumer doesn't get any satisfaction, loses their ongoing support and ends up with a very expensive doorstop. The only consolation is that it's a mistake that many people aren't likely to make twice.

Being forewarned about these very questionable products will provide you with some degree of awareness if you come across them.

Look for transparency

Look for system transparency. If I buy a readymade trading system, I want to know exactly how and why it works because I'm not going to risk my hard-earned money on some decision-making process that

I can't see or understand. My newsletters are simply a convenience product where we distil and bundle all the information you need into a single convenient package. In turn, I use other product and service providers to obtain the information I need to create my newsletters and I happily pay them for the convenience that they provide me. The processes that their programs employ are as transparent as the ones I use to create my newsletters. If I ask my product and service providers a question such as 'How do you calculate this ratio?' I expect to get a straight answer. I'm not saying I want to be given all the minute detail, down to their program's source code, but I do expect to be told the basic methodology being employed.

On the other hand, you may want to buy your own charting software and market data and do it all yourself. The choice is entirely up to you.

Derivative trading isn't easy

Another common hallmark of these 'off the shelf' trading solutions is they often attempt to fast track novice and would-be traders into dealing in sophisticated derivative products because this gives them the ability to sell the concept of leverage. There's no doubt that people will be attracted to an advertisement that offers an annual return of 200 per cent over an advertisement that offers only 20 per cent. The only way any trading system could possibly achieve these sorts of returns is with the aid of leverage.

Alternatively, you will see options trading programs that offer traders the ability to generate steady returns by 'selling' options to other traders. Options are a type of derivative. 'Selling' options is called option writing, where you become the issuer of the option and get paid a regular premium whenever you create and sell options. It carries a lower risk and lower return than buying and selling derivatives, but there are still risks and the science behind how the options market works is certainly not for the novice.

To give you a taste of what you need to understand to be a competent options trader, figure 14.1 shows the Black Scholes options pricing formula, which is the industry standard for pricing options here and overseas.

Figure 14.1: the Black Scholes options pricing formula

$$C(S, t) = N(d_1)\, S - N(d_2)\, Ke^{-r(T-t)}$$

$$d_1 = \frac{\ln(S/K) + (r + \frac{\sigma^2}{2})(T-t)}{\sigma\sqrt{T-t}}$$

$$d_2 = \frac{\ln(S/K) + (r - \frac{\sigma^2}{2})(T-t)}{\sigma\sqrt{T-t}}$$

Also,

$$d_2 = d_1 - \sigma\sqrt{T-t}$$

The price of a corresponding put option based on put-call parity is

$$P(S, t) = Ke^{-r(T-t)} - S + C(S, t)$$

$$= N(-d_2)\, Ke^{-r(T-t)} - N(-d_1)\, S.$$

- $N(\bullet)$ is the cumulative distribution function of the standard normal distribution
- $T-t$ is the time to maturity
- S is the spot price of the underlying asset
- K is the strike price
- r is the risk free rate (annual rate, expressed in terms of continuous compounding)
- σ is the volatility of returns of the underlying asset

If you think I'm trying to scare you, you're right. If you want to be a competent options trader, however, you need to get your head around this stuff. Of course, the trading systems vendors will tell you that their program does all the hard work for you so you don't have to make a single calculation. This may be the case, but you should still have a working understanding of what the program is doing for you.

In my newsletters we do all the risk management calculations for you, but I still maintain that any would-be share trader who isn't prepared to learn the theory behind risk management shouldn't be in the market (see discussion in chapter 4). My car includes an impressive array of automatic features such as automatic headlights, automatic wipers and cruise control, but I still have to understand and appreciate these systems to drive my car competently. The same goes for trading.

Take your time

Taking the analogy of driving a motor car and trading a step further: I learnt to drive a car in a carpark, not on a racetrack, and trading financial markets is no different. Trading fully paid ordinary shares is where all traders should begin their journey. When you've succeeded at trading shares, you can start to contemplate trading other types of financial products.

In summary, here are the important points to remember.

- Trading involves wins and losses, and mastering your losses makes you successful. Few traders will publicly talk about their losses, however, and dubious product and service providers will never mention them.

- The media doesn't know anything that you don't know about what's going to happen in the future.

- We need to use stockbrokers to trade, but make sure you choose a stockbroker as opposed to having a stockbroker choose you.

- There's no such thing as an 'everything' trader. If you try to become one you'll probably end up a 'nothing' trader.

Stay focused, stick to what you know and start at the beginning. In the last chapter that's where I'll take you—back to the beginning by trading blue chip shares.

Chapter 15

Blue chip share trading

Although this book is essentially about two short-term trading strategies, I keep mentioning blue chip share trading—and for good reason. Blue chip shares are the elephants of the stock market because they move relatively slowly and usually exhibit a lack of volatility. They are the most predictable and easiest shares to trade, so blue chip share trading is considered to be the kindergarten of trading.

I recommend that novice share traders learn to trade, at least in part, by trading blue chip shares. You will inevitably suffer losses and it's best if these losses are kept relatively small. As discussed in chapter 13, you learn to trade through the pain you endure by losing money and not by making it—but this doesn't mean that you have to suffer big losses.

Capital allocation

The trick is to temper your pace by trading with a mix of short-term and longer term trading strategies. I'll reiterate my recommendation about capital allocation from chapter 4, where I suggest putting two parts of your trading capital in blue chip shares for every one part you put in short-term, medium risk strategies:

- 67 per cent low risk—my active investing strategy for blue chip shares

- 33 per cent medium risk—my active trading and breakout trading strategies.

My active investing strategy (see chapter 5) is the obvious blue chip companion product to both the shorter term, medium-risk strategies explained in this book. The indicator set and trading process are almost identical to the active trading strategy, with the only major difference being the inclusion of fundamental analysis.

Like its little brother, active trading, the active investing strategy requires a fair degree of discretionary input by the user, largely through the interpretation of MMA charts. This is a key filter used in both systems to eliminate volatility and locate shares in steady upward (or downward) trends. But this discretionary aspect may not suit your personality and temperament, so I'm going to offer you an alternative blue chip share trading strategy.

Active fund management

Active fund management (AFM) strategy is a mechanical adaptation of active investing where the use of MMA chart interpretation has been completely eliminated. Rather, it relies on a set of very robust filters and indicators that virtually mechanise the entire trading process. The basic premise behind this strategy is still the same as that of active investing—to seek out fundamentally sound shares that are rising in price.

The simplicity of this system is evident at the outset, where rather than use a two-stage filter like active investing with its fundamental and rate of return searches, the AFM strategy uses just one search routine. Using the ASX200 constituent shares as its universe, the AFM strategy simply applies an appropriately tuned rate of annual return indicator to all 200 shares, then puts them in descending order, according to their rate of annual return.

In other words, the fastest rising shares (that is, the most profitable ones) are at the top of the list while the least profitable (the ones that are trending down) are at the bottom. By doing this we can easily scoop off the 10 most profitable shares from the top of the list to create a portfolio of blue chip shares. The list in figure 15.1 is an example taken from my weekly *Blue chip report*, showing the top 15 shares. Note the rate of annual return (ROAR) column is in descending order.

Figure 15.1: top 15 blue chip shares

ASX200 Search Results

Code	Company Name	Price($)	ROAR(%)	Cashflow($)	Industry Group	Stop Loss($)
LNC	Linc Energy	2.95	97.52	1352713	Energy	2.38
ILU	Iluka Resources	13.50	94.21	7345301	Materials	10.80
AGO	Atlas Iron	3.84	74.69	6620625	Materials	3.18
RIV	Riversdale Mining	16.52	72.79	6659474	Energy	13.60
MML	Medusa Mining	8.00	71.66	1801546	Materials	6.40
BLY	Boart Longyear	4.78	62.52	3633367	Capital Goods	3.88
MND	Monadelphous Group	21.53	56.01	1661953	Capital Goods	17.92
MIN	Mineral Resources	12.50	55.10	1543206	Materials	10.78
CTX	Caltex Aust.	15.33	53.59	3146334	Energy	12.67
AWC	Alumina	2.70	52.65	9861524	Materials	2.16
PRU	Perseus Mining	3.39	52.07	1253812	Materials	2.71
IPL	Incitec Pivot	4.43	48.97	10153198	Materials	3.70
FMG	Fortescue Metals Group	6.72	47.99	22511158	Materials	5.50
OZL	OZ Minerals	1.65	46.80	7908750	Materials	1.42
WSA	Western Areas Mining	7.16	43.45	1335205	Materials	5.73

This strategy assumes that if a share is included in the Standard and Poor's ASX200 index it must have reasonable fundamentals. It's not an overly discerning approach when it comes to fundamental analysis, but the idea is to keep the process as simple and as robust as possible.

Having put all the ASX200 shares in order of their profitability, we take the top 10 shares to create our portfolio. Next, we have to actively manage this portfolio on a week-by-week basis.

Optimisation

The first step in managing our portfolio is to ensure that it is constantly being optimised and we aren't hanging on to any shares that are beginning to slow. We want our money to be working hard for us and this means we have to continually cull the dead wood. This concept is easily explained graphically by taking several shares that are trending—two that are trending up and two that are trending down. The diagram in figure 15.2 depicts these four trending shares (black lines), along with an index (grey line) which is the average of these four trends.

Figure 15.2: four trending shares and their average or index

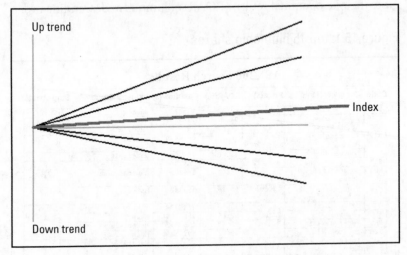

If we eliminate the two shares that are trending down, the average performance, defined by the index, will improve considerably. Figure 15.3 shows what we have after we've optimised these four shares.

Figure 15.3: the two rising shares and their average or index

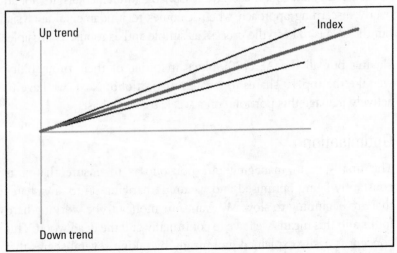

We optimise our active fund management 10 share portfolio by selling off any shares that fall outside the top 40 on our list and replacing them with shares from the top of the list. We are therefore constantly ensuring that our money is working as hard as it possibly can.

The next thing we have to do is apply a trailing stop loss. The objective with this strategy is to keep it as simple and as robust as possible, so it makes sense to apply a very wide stop loss that can absorb a lot of volatility.

Drawdown stop loss

Introducing the drawdown stop loss, which is created by subtracting a fixed percentage from the highest closing price in an uptrending market. The value of the drawdown stop loss is not allowed to fall back with price activity, so a line that looks like an uneven staircase is generated. Figure 15.4 shows the chart of CSL, which experienced a long-term trend that lasted for nearly six years. It is shown with a 20 per cent drawdown stop loss applied.

Figure 15.4: six-year chart of CSL with a 20 per cent drawdown stop loss

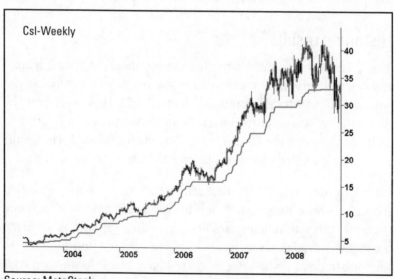

Source: MetaStock

You can see in this example of CSL that the 20 per cent drawdown stop loss is ideally suited for managing these really big, medium- to long-term trends. On the other hand, a sensitive stop loss such as the MACD indicator, which we use in the breakout trading strategy, would be completely inappropriate in this situation. It's a case of using the right tool for the right job.

The 2 per cent risk rule

If a share is stopped out, we sell it and replace it with a share from the top of our list, in exactly the same way as we do when we're optimising. But here's the really clever bit: by applying a 20 per cent drawdown stop loss to each share and having our money spread across 10 shares, we are applying the 2 per cent risk rule— 20 per cent of 10 per cent is 2 per cent. If one of our shares is stopped out, our largest possible loss from that position is 2 per cent of our total capital.

This has been a fairly brief tour of my active fund management strategy which, as I explained earlier, is a mechanical adaptation of the active investing strategy. When asked to differentiate between the two approaches I use the analogy of driving a car, where the active investing strategy is a manual transmission and the active fund management strategy is an automatic transmission.

Historical results

The AFM strategy is entirely mechanical and therefore doesn't require any discretionary input on the part of the user, so I can provide you with a set of backtested results (see figure 15.5). They show how the AFM strategy has performed over the nine-year period from 2001 to 2010, compared to the ASX200 index on which it is based. The results are broken into financial years, which run from 1 July to 30 June.

I can't supply results for the active trading or active investing strategies because these systems rely heavily on discretion and therefore they will generate different results, depending on who is applying them. Even though there is some degree of discretion required in selecting trades, I do have historical results available for my breakout trading strategy available on my website at <www.alanhull.com>. You will also find a detailed explanation of the active fund management strategy, available in a 40-page downloadable pdf file.

Figure 15.5: backtested AFM strategy results

Cumulative performance comparison				
	S&P ASX200 Index		Active Fund Management	
July 2001		$100,000		$100,000
2001/2002	-7.9%	$92,100	7.6%	$107,600
2002/2003	-5.8%	$86,758	11.3%	$119,759
2003/2004	16.8%	$101,333	48.6%	$177,962
2004/2005	21.1%	$122,714	58.0%	$281,180
2005/2006	18.7%	$145,662	26.0%	$354,287
2006/2007	23.7%	$180,184	38.7%	$491,396
2007/2008	-16.9%	$147,931	6.1%	$521,371
2008/2009	-24.2%	$112,132	-18.2%	$426,481
2009/2010	8.8%	$122,000	-11.9%	$375,730

- These results do not include external costs such as taxation, etc
- Please note that past performance is no guarantee of future returns
- This simulation is a guide only and has not been independently audited

The market will teach you

A comprehensive range of trading strategies is available when it comes to share trading, and now I've shown you how to trade my way by exposing you to every trading system that I personally use to trade Australian shares. Share trading is a journey of self-discovery, however, where you need to shop around and be willing to try different approaches until you find what works for you.

I can provide you with trading systems I know are profitable, but I can't tell you what strategy is right for your psychology, lifestyle and objectives. The only person who can answer that question is you. You may shop around and try out different trading systems, but please remember the one piece of advice that made me successful: never risk more than 2 per cent of total capital on any individual trade.

Ultimately, it is the market that teaches us all how to trade. The trick is to survive long enough to learn the lessons.

Appendix A

MetaStock indicator formulae for active trading

Index crossover charts (daily charts)

10-day exponential moving average—grey

30-day exponential moving average—black

Multiple moving average (MMA) charts (weekly charts)

Exponential moving averages (EMA):

Short-term group (grey) periods 3, 5, 7, 9, 11, 13

Long-term group (black) periods 21, 24, 27, 30, 33, 36

Hull moving average (HMA) (use indicator builder)

period:=Input("period",1,200,20);   *where the default value for period is 20*

sqrtperiod:=Sqrt(period);

Mov(2*Mov(C,period/2,W) - Mov(C,period,W),LastValue (sqrtperiod),W);

RoR indicator (rate of annual return for weekly charts)

Using 26-period Hull moving average:

400*((Mov(2*Mov(C,13,W) − Mov(C,26,W),LastValue(Sqrt(26)),W))
−ref((Mov(2*Mov(C,13,W) − Mov(C,26,W),LastValue(Sqrt(26)),W)),
−13))/(Mov(2*Mov(C,13,W) − Mov(C,26,W),LastValue(Sqrt(26)),W));

where a share's entry ROAR = 120% and its exit ROAR = 80%

Range indicator (weekly charts)

Using eight-period Hull moving average:

Central cord

(Mov(2*Mov(H,4,W) − Mov(H,8,W),LastValue(Sqrt(8)),W));

Lower deviation

If((Mov(2*Mov(H,4,W) − Mov(H,8,W),LastValue(Sqrt(8)),W))> PREV, (If((Mov(2*Mov(H,4,W) − Mov(H,8,W), LastValue(Sqrt(8)), W)) − (2*ATR(4))>PREV, (Mov(2*Mov(H,4,W) − Mov(H,8,W), LastValue(Sqrt(8)),W))−(2*ATR(4)), PREV)), (Mov(2*Mov(H,4,W) − Mov(H,8,W), LastValue(Sqrt(8)),W)));

Upper deviation

(Mov(2*Mov(H,4,W) − Mov(H,8,W),LastValue(Sqrt(8)),W))+ (2*ATR(8));

Appendix B
MetaStock indicator formulae for breakout trading

Following are some MetaStock codes that may be of use for some quantitative measures in a breakout trading strategy.

Breakout to the upside

Volatility measure = close of breakout candle is above the previous candle by more than half the ATR (17)

$Close > (Ref (Close,-1) + (0.5 * ATR (17)))$

Closing price position = close of breakout candle is above its midpoint

$Close > (Low + ((H-L) * 0.5))$

MACD measure = at the breakout, the MACD line is above its signal line and rising

$MACD () > Ref (MACD (), -1) AND MACD () > Mov (MACD (), 9, E)$

Closing price magnitude = close of the breakout candle is greater than 20 cents to help ensure there is sufficient liquidity

$Close > 0.2$ *{this will depend on what unit your price data uses}*

Trailing stop loss = displacement of 2 times ATR (17) below the highest high during the trading. Include a statement to ensure the trailing stop loss only rises during the trade.

*Displacement:=HHV(HIGH - (2 * ATR(17)), 5);*

Stop:= If(Ref(CLOSE, -1)>PREV AND Displacement<PREV, PREV, Displacement);

{Plot the Stop Loss}

Stop;

Entry limit = 2.5 × ATR (17) above the trailing stop loss *at the breakout only*

*Limit:= Stop + (2.5 * ATR(17));*

Breakout to the downside

Volatility measure = close of breakout candle is below the previous candle by more than half the ATR (17)

*Close < (Ref (Close,-1) − (0.5 * ATR (17)))*

Closing price position = close of breakout candle is below its midpoint

*Close < (High − ((H-L) * 0.5))*

MACD measure = at the breakout, the MACD line is below its signal line and falling

MACD () < Ref (MACD (), -1) AND MACD () < Mov (MACD (), 9, E)

Closing price magnitude = close of the breakout candle is greater than $1 to help ensure there is still enough room above zero for the price to continue falling for a reasonable period

Close > 1   {this will depend on what unit your price data uses}

Trailing stop loss = displacement of 2 × ATR (17) above the lowest low during the trading. Include a statement to ensure the trailing stop loss only falls during the trade.

*Displacement:=LLV(LOW + (2 * ATR(17)), 5);*

Stop:=If(Ref(CLOSE, -1)<PREV AND Displacement>PREV, PREV, Displacement);

{Plot the Stop Loss}

Stop;

Entry limit = 2.5 × ATR (17) below the trailing stop loss *at the breakout only*

*Limit:=Stop − (2.5 * ATR(17));*

Appendix C
Trading performance and strategy review

This process should be undertaken every six months, providing at least 30 trades have been executed, with one trade including both a market entry and exit. Otherwise, it should be done at least every 12 months. The guidelines given here are of a very general nature and you may wish to further refine and tailor this generic template to better suit your own personal requirements.

Results since last review

Starting date   ____/____/____

Starting capital $_____

Final date   ____/____/____

Final capital $_____

Annualised return   _____%

Number of winning trades   _____

Number of losing trades   _____

Average winning trade $_____

Average losing trade $_____

Average winning and losing trades should include brokerage costs

Expectancy   _____

Expectancy = (probability of winning × avg win/avg loss)
            − probability of losing

where the probability of winning and losing are expressed as fractions. Refer to chapter 4 for a detailed explanation of expectancy.

Am I happy with the above results?   Yes / No

If you are happy, then go no further!

Strategy review
Trading premise

Comments

_____

_____

_____

_____

Changes/improvements

_____

_____

_____

_____

Trading conditions

(for example, is the broader market trending up or down?)

Comments

_____

_____

_____

_____

Changes/improvements

_____

_____

_____

_____

Search procedure(s)

Comments

_____

_____

_____

_____

Changes/improvements

_____

_____

_____

Trade entry

Comments

_____

_____

_____

_____

Changes/improvements

_____

_____

_____

Trade exit

Comments

_____

_____

_____

_____

Changes/improvements

_____

_____

_____

_____

Risk management

Comments

_____

_____

_____

_____

Changes/improvements

_____

_____

_____

_____

Summary of changes

_____

_____

_____

_____

Index

ActTrade newsletter subscription form

The *ActTrade* newsletter is updated every week and is available to download over the weekend.

The *ActTrade* newsletter includes:

- the All Ordinaries and Small Ordinaries crossover charts
- sector MMA charts and rate of return values
- weekly rate of return search results of the entire ASX
- all range indicator values and portfolio weightings for the two per cent risk rule of shares that have passed the weekly rate of return search
- MMA charts of shares that have passed the weekly rate of return search.

Please print all details clearly, tick where appropriate, sign, date and fax or post to:

ActVest P/L

53 Grange Drive

Lysterfield

Victoria, 3156

or fax 03 9778 7062

Please forward your enquiries to enquiries@alanhull.com

YES ☐   I wish to subscribe to the *ActTrade* newsletter at $33.00 per month plus an initial joining fee of $49.50 AND receive, as a bonus, the ActVest Trade Recorder for FREE (valued at $49.50)

Please charge to my credit card: VISA ☐ MasterCard ☐

Card no. __ __ __ __   __ __ __ __   __ __ __ __   Expiry: __ / __

Full name _____

Email address _____

Daytime phone _____

Please sign here .... Date: /   /

I understand that signing this form indicates my acceptance of the terms and conditions contained overleaf.

DISCLAIMER

- Alan Hull is an authorised representative of Gryphon Learning, holder of Australian Financial Services Licence No. 246606. None of Gryphon Learning Pty Ltd, its Authorised Representatives, the 'Gryphon System', 'Gryphon MultiMedia', and 'Gryphon Scanner' take into account the investment objectives, financial situation and particular needs of any particular person and before making an investment decision on the basis of the 'Gryphon System', 'Gryphon MultiMedia' and 'Gryphon Scanner' or any of its authorised representatives, a prospective investor needs to consider with or without the assistance of a securities adviser, whether the advice is appropriate in the light of the particular investment needs, objectives and financial circumstances of the prospective investor.

- Although every care is taken the nature and content of the education and/or training prevents the giving or making of any representations or guarantees as to the commercial or financial suitability of any of the material, information and opinions given.

- Alan Hull and his servants and/or agents accept no liability for any reliance upon the material, information and opinion given in any course or written materials and no responsibility is accepted for any losses, charges, damages or expenses which may be sustained or incurred by any participant or otherwise by reason of any reliance upon the materials, information or opinion given.

- Individuals are responsible for making their own assessment of all materials provided and are hereby expressly advised to verify and to obtain independent advice before acting on any representations, statements, information or opinions given.

- This disclaimer is a continuing disclaimer and applies to the primary course or written materials provided and any future support given (whether on-going or otherwise).

Acknowledgement

- I, the abovesigned, acknowledge that I have read and understand the above advice and disclaimer.

- I acknowledge that ActVest P/L ABN 44 101 040 939 must retain my credit card details for the purpose of charging me $33.00 including GST on the 1st day of each month for my *ActTrade* newsletter subscription and that, should I elect to discontinue my subscription, I must notify ActVest P/L in writing.

- I acknowledge that I will at all times in the future indemnify Alan Hull and his servants and/or agents against all actions, liabilities, proceedings, claims, costs and expenses which I may suffer, incur, or sustain in connection with, or arising in any way whatsoever in reliance upon any material, information or opinions provided by Alan Hull and his servants and/or agents.

- I acknowledge that any future dealings I may undertake in any securities will be entered into freely and voluntarily and without inducement or encouragement from Alan Hull and his servants and/or agents.

Breakout trading newsletter subscription form

The *Breakout trading* newsletter is updated every week and is available to download over the weekend.

The *Breakout trading* newsletter will provide you with:

- charts of all new and existing long and short trades
- entry and exit data including specific buy, hold and sell signals
- all risk management calculations....

...so you can implement the strategy in less than an hour a week!

Please print all details clearly, tick where appropriate, sign, date and fax or post to:

ActVest P/L

53 Grange Drive

Lysterfield

Victoria, 3156

or fax 03 9778 7062

Please forward your enquiries to enquiries@alanhull.com

YES ☐   I wish to subscribe to the *Breakout trading* newsletter at $49.50 per month plus an initial joining fee of $49.50 AND receive, as a bonus, the ActVest Trade Recorder FREE (valued at $49.50)

Please charge to my credit card: Visa ☐   Mastercard ☐

Card no. _ _ _ _   _ _ _ _   _ _   Expiry date: _ / _

Full name _____

Email address _____

Daytime phone _____

Please sign here .... Date: / /

I understand that signing this form indicates my acceptance of the terms and conditions contained overleaf.

DISCLAIMER

- Alan Hull is an authorised representative of Gryphon Learning, holder of Australian Financial Services Licence No. 246606. None of Gryphon Learning Pty Ltd, its Authorised Representatives, the 'Gryphon System', 'Gryphon MultiMedia', and 'Gryphon Scanner' take into account the investment objectives, financial situation and particular needs of any particular person and before making an investment decision on the basis of the 'Gryphon System', 'Gryphon MultiMedia' and 'Gryphon Scanner' or any of its authorised representatives, a prospective investor needs to consider with or without the assistance of a securities adviser, whether the advice is appropriate in the light of the particular investment needs, objectives and financial circumstances of the prospective investor.

- Although every care is taken the nature and content of the education and/or training prevents the giving or making of any representations or guarantees as to the commercial or financial suitability of any of the material, information and opinions given.

- Alan Hull and his servants and/or agents accept no liability for any reliance upon the material, information and opinion given in any course or written materials and no responsibility is accepted for any losses, charges, damages or expenses which may be sustained or incurred by any participant or otherwise by reason of any reliance upon the materials, information or opinion given.

- Individuals are responsible for making their own assessment of all materials provided and are hereby expressly advised to verify and to obtain independent advice before acting on any representations, statements, information or opinions given.

- This disclaimer is a continuing disclaimer and applies to the primary course or written materials provided and any future support given (whether on-going or otherwise).

Acknowledgement

- I, the abovesigned, acknowledge that I have read and understand the above advice and disclaimer.

- I acknowledge that ActVest P/L ABN 44 101 040 939 must retain my credit card details for the purpose of charging me $49.50 including GST on the 1st day of each month for my *Breakout trading* newsletter subscription and that, should I elect to discontinue my subscription, I must notify ActVest P/L in writing.

- I acknowledge that I will at all times in the future indemnify Alan Hull and his servants and/or agents against all actions, liabilities, proceedings, claims, costs and expenses which I may suffer, incur, or sustain in connection with, or arising in any way whatsoever in reliance upon any material, information or opinions provided by Alan Hull and his servants and/or agents.

- I acknowledge that any future dealings I may undertake in any securities will be entered into freely and voluntarily and without inducement or encouragement from Alan Hull and his servants and/or agents.

Also in this trading series

Available from all good bookstores